Nowhere in the world is Taylor Woodrow's environmental stewardship more evident than in its communities and homes throughout Florida. We celebrate the state's natural treasures, and hope that you will enjoy this beautiful collection of Florida landscape photography by Clyde Butcher.

Taylor Woodrow has been developing lifestyle communities and building luxury homes and condominiums for over 80 years. One of Europe's largest homebuilders, Taylor Woodrow builds over 13,000 homes worldwide each year. The North American division of this internationally recognized company has more than 100 active developments throughout Florida, California, Arizona, Texas and Canada.

Our commitment to architectural excellence and unsurpassed quality is showcased in every community and home that bears our name. Taylor Woodrow has a long and distinguished record of giving back to the communities in which we build. Equally important to us is a deep and abiding respect for the environment. We are committed to being a conscientious developer and homebuilder, making the most efficient use of land during the planning process and protecting and enhancing the environment wherever possible.

Thank you again for selecting a Taylor Woodrow home.
It is our pleasure to welcome you.

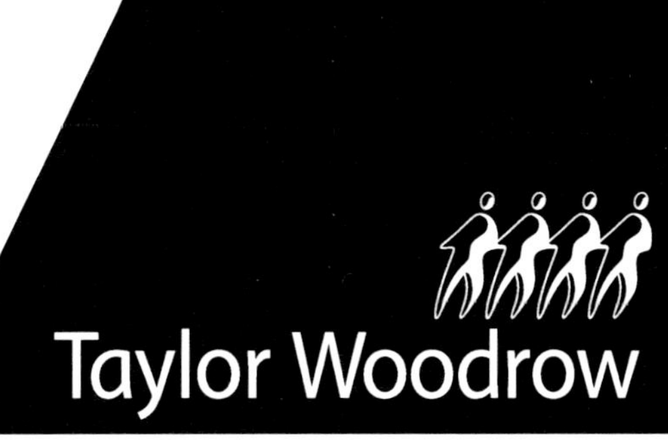

CLYDE BUTCHER
FLORIDA LANDSCAPE

This book is dedicated to my daughter, Jackie.
Her love and joy for life has been my inspiration. She has given me courage in dark days, and brought light into my life. I have been fortunate to have her in my life.

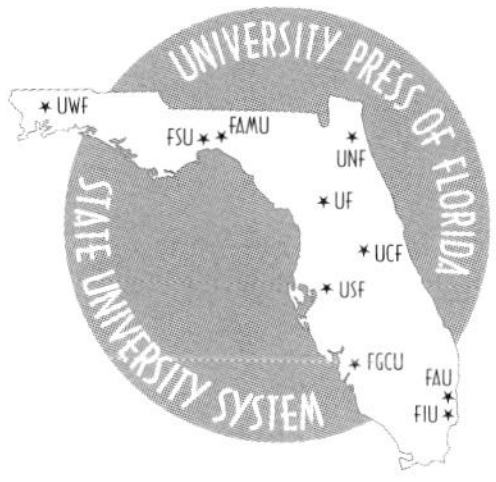

Florida A&M University, Tallahassee
Florida Atlantic University, Boca Raton
Florida Gulf Coast University, Ft. Myers
Florida International University, Miami
Florida State University, Tallahassee
University of Central Florida, Orlando
University of Florida, Gainesville
University of North Florida, Jacksonville
University of South Florida, Tampa
University of West Florida, Pensacola

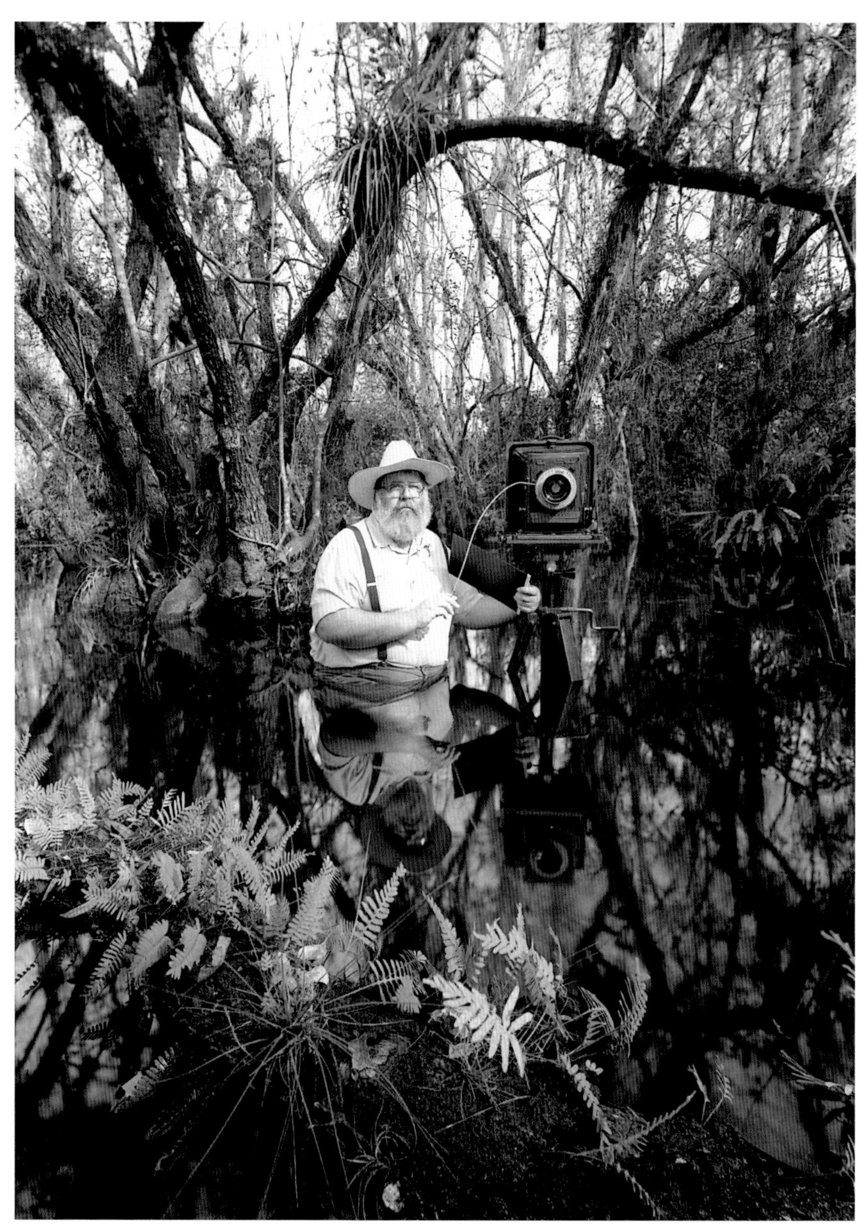

Photo by Woody Walters

FLORIDA

I came to Florida in 1980 as a sailor. We had raised our children aboard a sailboat, and Florida offered a myriad of sailing opportunities. We were attracted to the warm water and tropical breezes, however, I saw nothing in Florida that was worth photographing. When I wanted to photograph I would travel back west in search of stunning western vistas.

My attitude toward Florida changed dramatically in 1983, when Niki and I stopped to visit the quaint Ma & Pa roadside attraction called Tom Gaskin's Cypress Knee Museum. We walked along Tom's boardwalk into the swamp that bordered Fisheating Creek. The primeval beauty of the cypress forest stunned me. It had the same feeling of eternity that I felt when I am in the Redwood forest. I fell in love. I went back the next day with my camera and photographed what I had felt, and I have been photographing Florida ever since.

With my eyes now wide open to the beauty of Florida, I became aware of the need to get into it, however, the environment of Florida is somewhat intimidating! How was I going to get the courage to hike out into waist deep water amidst snakes and alligators to capture the images I wanted? It was then that a gift of friendship was given to me, and I met Oscar Thompson, a fifth generation native of South Florida. He became my guide and friend as we adventured into the wilds of Florida. He taught me that although the environment in Florida is unique, it is not something that should cause fear. We have spent many years together photographing and traipsing through the backcountry and islands of Florida. The adventure has changed my life.

My awareness of the population growth and the rapid disappearance of natural Florida began to worry me. Suddenly my photographs of Florida were becoming history rather than images of how Florida presently appeared. That knowledge was very disturbing, and motivated me to begin my conservation activities. Saving the Everglades by working with state agencies and national environmental groups has become a major part of my life. Through the use of my images, I hope the people of Florida have come to a greater understanding of the beauty they will lose if the preservation and restoration of our environment is not in the forefront of our thoughts. As people of Florida, we must establish an ethic toward the earth that will penetrate the very soul of our existence. One that will lead the way toward a connection to nature in a deep and personal way, so that other states and countries may follow our lead.

As an artist, I reach deep within myself in order to express an image that will touch another. Art is an intimate experience. It is with this intimate experience that I believe the artist has the power to transform and bring a new insight into life. I believe artists are vessels of inspiration, and it is my hope that the vision I give to you of Florida will inspire you to love and protect the environment for generations to come.

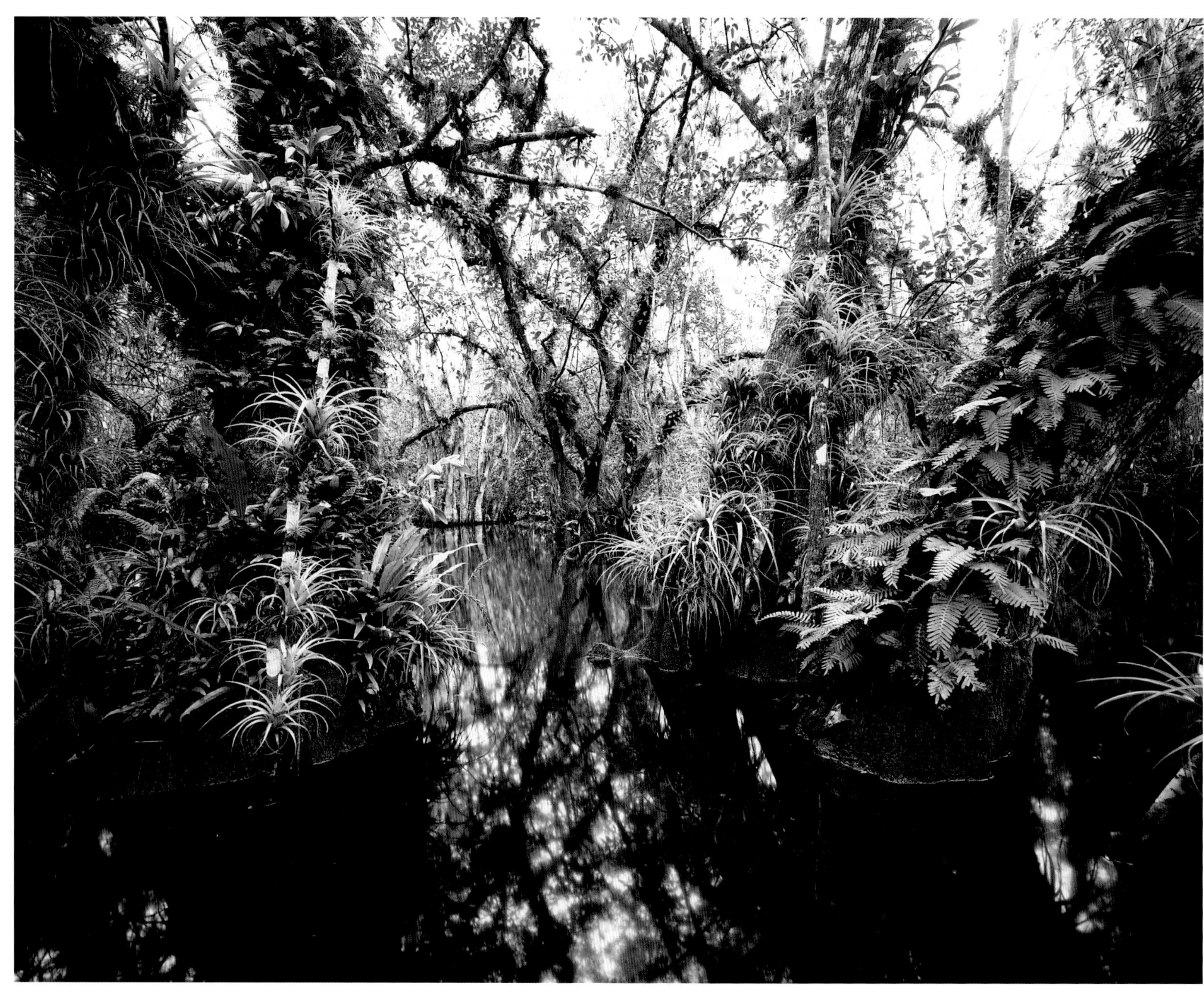

Loosescrew Sanctuary #2
Plate 1

INTRODUCTION

By Mr. Bob Bendick
Vice-President and Florida Chapter Director of The Nature Conservancy

On a day my daughter, Robin, was to return to college, we went canoeing on a wild Florida river close to the city where we live. It was raining, but the canopy of trees kept us from getting wet. Because of the weather, there was no one else on the river. We saw an otter swimming beneath the clear, spring-fed water, and wood storks feeding along the shore. Alligators splashed from the banks, and we heard the strange cry of the limpkin. As we were returning to the landing at the end of the day, we passed a tree that had recently fallen into the river. One of its branches was moving slowly back and forth against the pressure of the otherwise imperceptible current. My daughter watched the branch. "It is," she said, "like the heartbeat of the river."

For much of the year in Florida there is a surfeit of crickets, a chorus such that it is impossible to tell one from another. But one autumn, when we lived in upstate New York, a single cricket made its way inside our house. It took to chirping on cold, gray afternoons when the children built a fire in the hearth and the north wind swirled dry leaves across the pavement in front of the garage. It is not unusual for crickets to find their way into houses in the fall. The cricket's daily song was not a particularly strange event, but I found it a sign of hope, of the determination of life to prevail even against a certain end. I remember the slow rhythm of its song today.

The branch in the river could easily have gone unnoticed. I might have ignored the cricket's voice, but I did not because it resonated within me. Just as true love requires two lovers, and lightning strikes from the ground up and the sky down, our relationship with the natural world originates both from within us and from nature itself. The magic of Clyde Butcher's exceptional photographs draw us in, help us to see nature in a new, clearer light. Each image is a story, a product of time, of seed falling, a tree growing and falling, a storm coming and leaving cool, smoking mist, a plant pushing out another plant, the rays of the sun crossing the blackness of space. The images have depth. It is as if they are open doorways. And there is something about the juxtaposition of sky, land and water that renews one's wonder about how the story depicted in the photographs was written, about the unrepeatable sequence of events that produced live oaks and wildflowers. Are the places Clyde reveals to us solely a product of the processes of geology and evolution, or is there more beyond those billowing clouds?

Whatever the origin of the immense diversity of life on our planet, it shouldn't change how we should act. We should save what has been created. But the saving will take a long time. Generations. We must rely on our daughters and our sons to carry conservation on into the future, but they will not save what they don't love and they will not love what they don't know.

So we must step with them through Clyde's doorways, to walk together up to our knees in the dark, tannin-stained water of the swamp, to be afraid of what might be there, to be grateful to be home, to want to go back. And in the evening we should sit with our children on the front porch, sit with them and turn the pages of Clyde's books by the light of the table lamp, assure them that, with their help, his images of nature are not a record of what was, but a representation of their inheritance, tell them that conservation is not some thankless chore, something to be left to bureaucrats, but an adventure for us all, a journey in shaping the future that can bind us together through shared adversity and tangible, lasting accomplishment.

We should close the book and turn off the light and sit with them and watch flashes of lightning in the distance, and listen to the wind from the lake rustling in the cabbage palms and hear the chorus of the cricket frogs and the back and forth hooting of the barred owls, the rustling of living things out there in the darkness beyond the edge of the lawn. In time, then, our children and theirs will remember that we sat and turned these pages with them. They will remember and be grateful and think of us when the night wind blows from the lake.

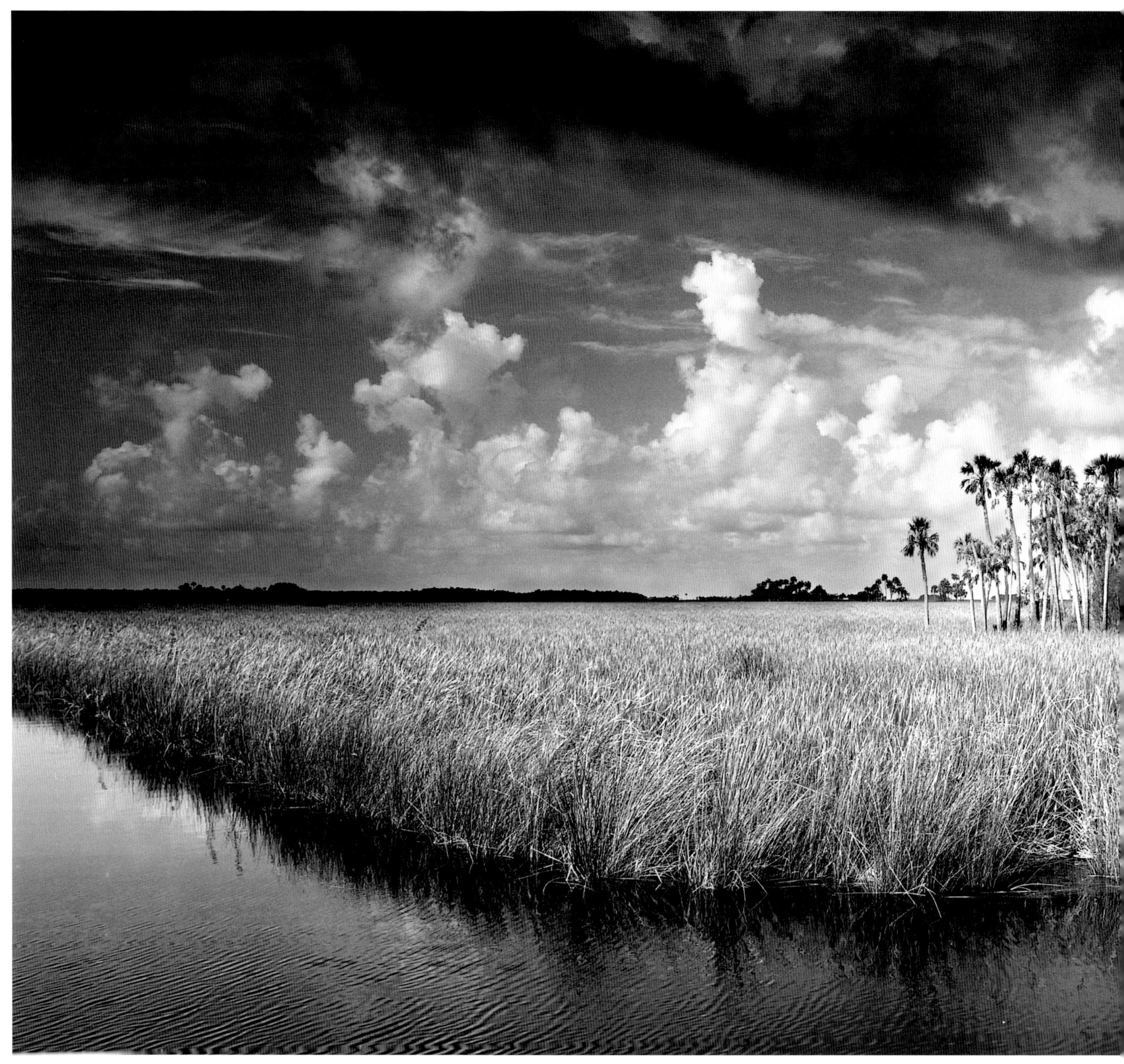

Seven Cabbage Cut   Plate 2

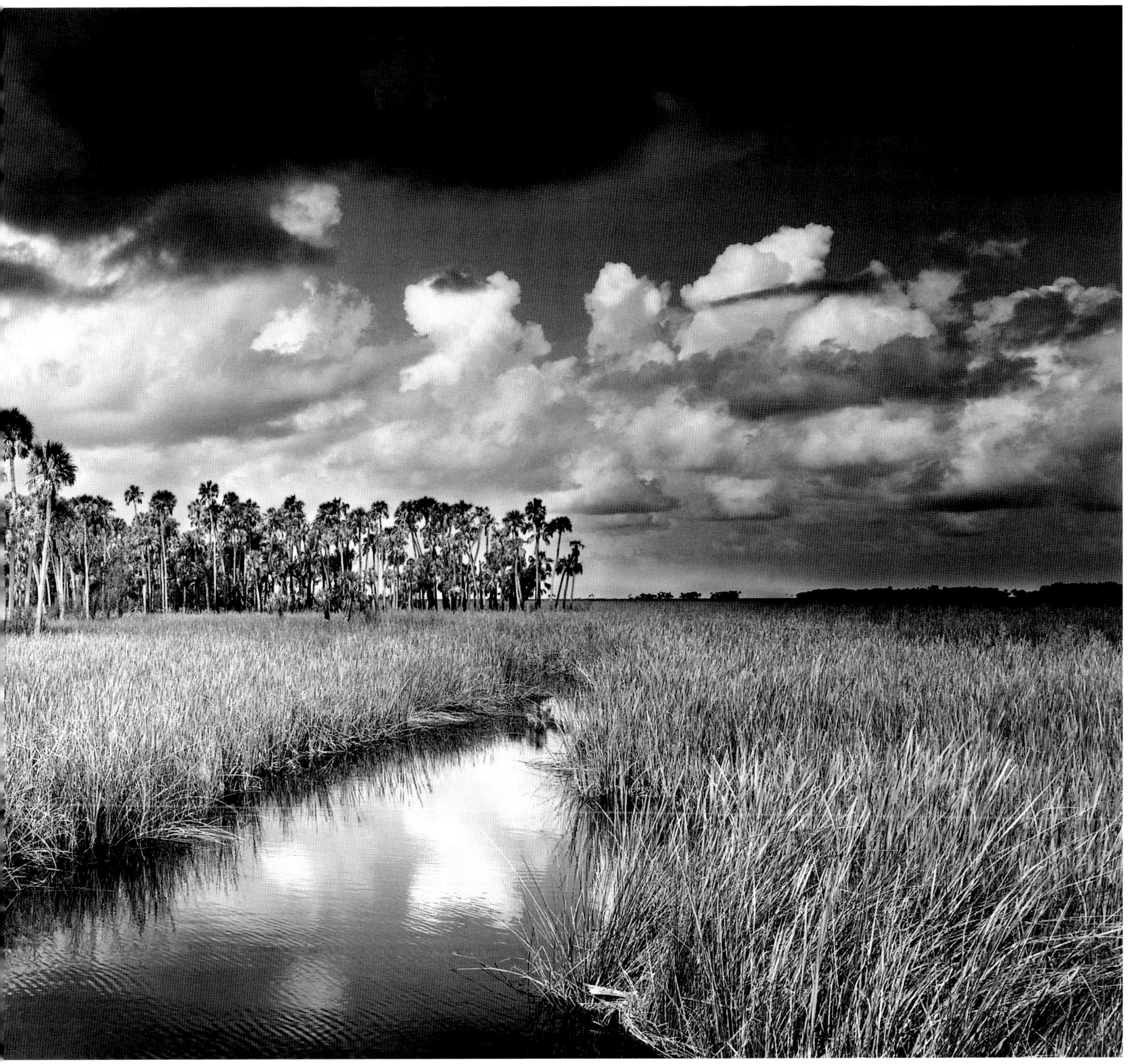

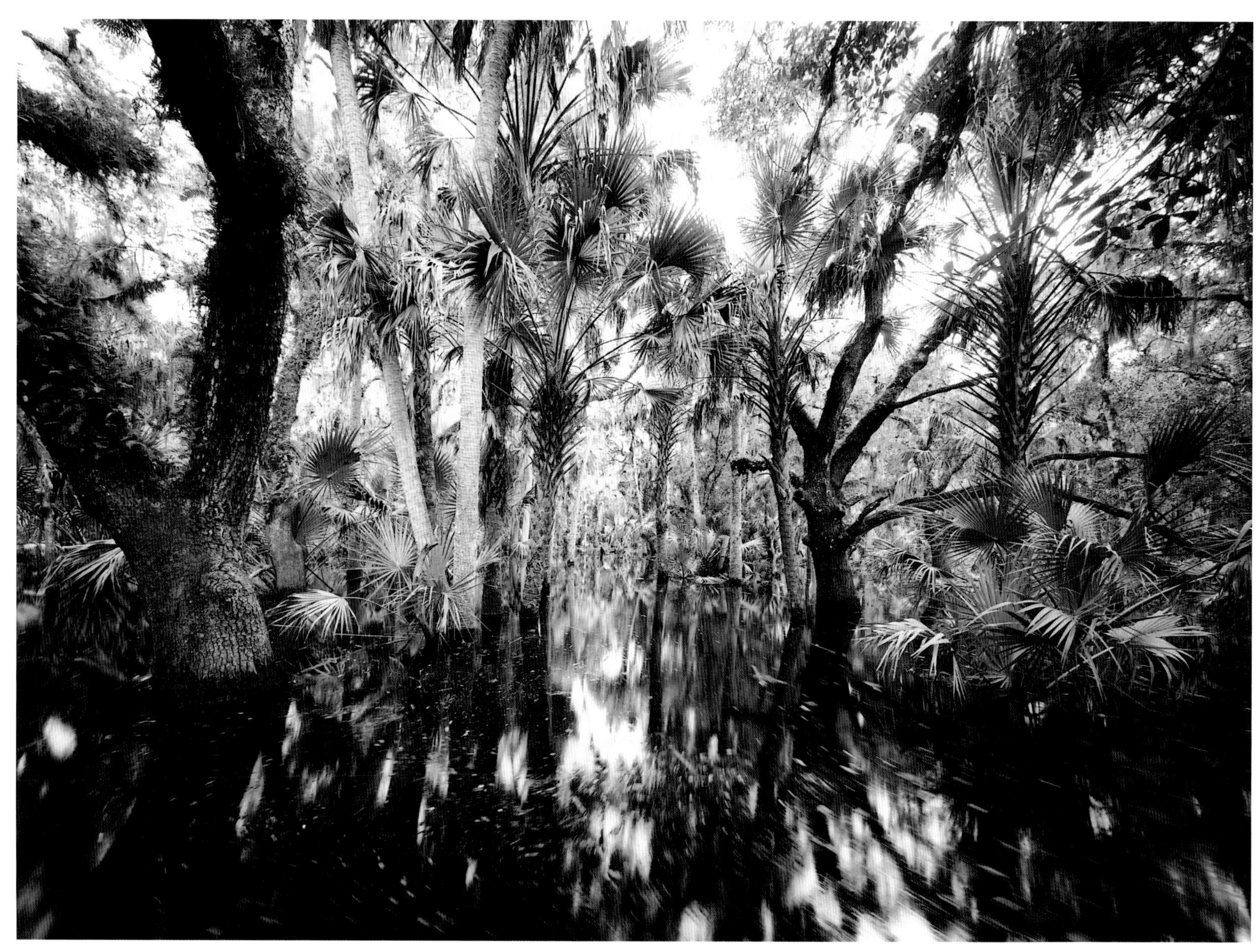

Myakka Canopy Trail
Plate 3

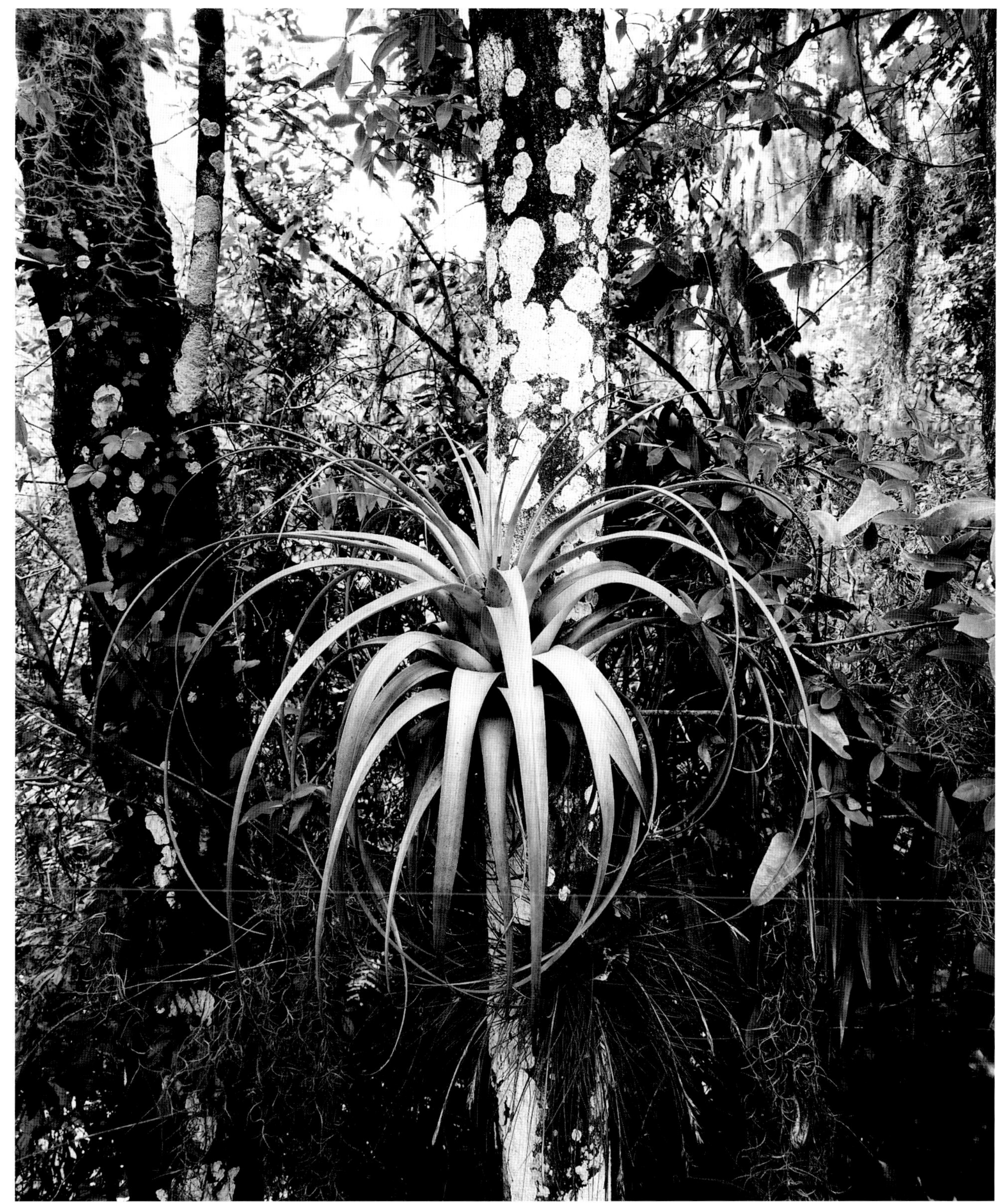

Myakka #5
Plate 4

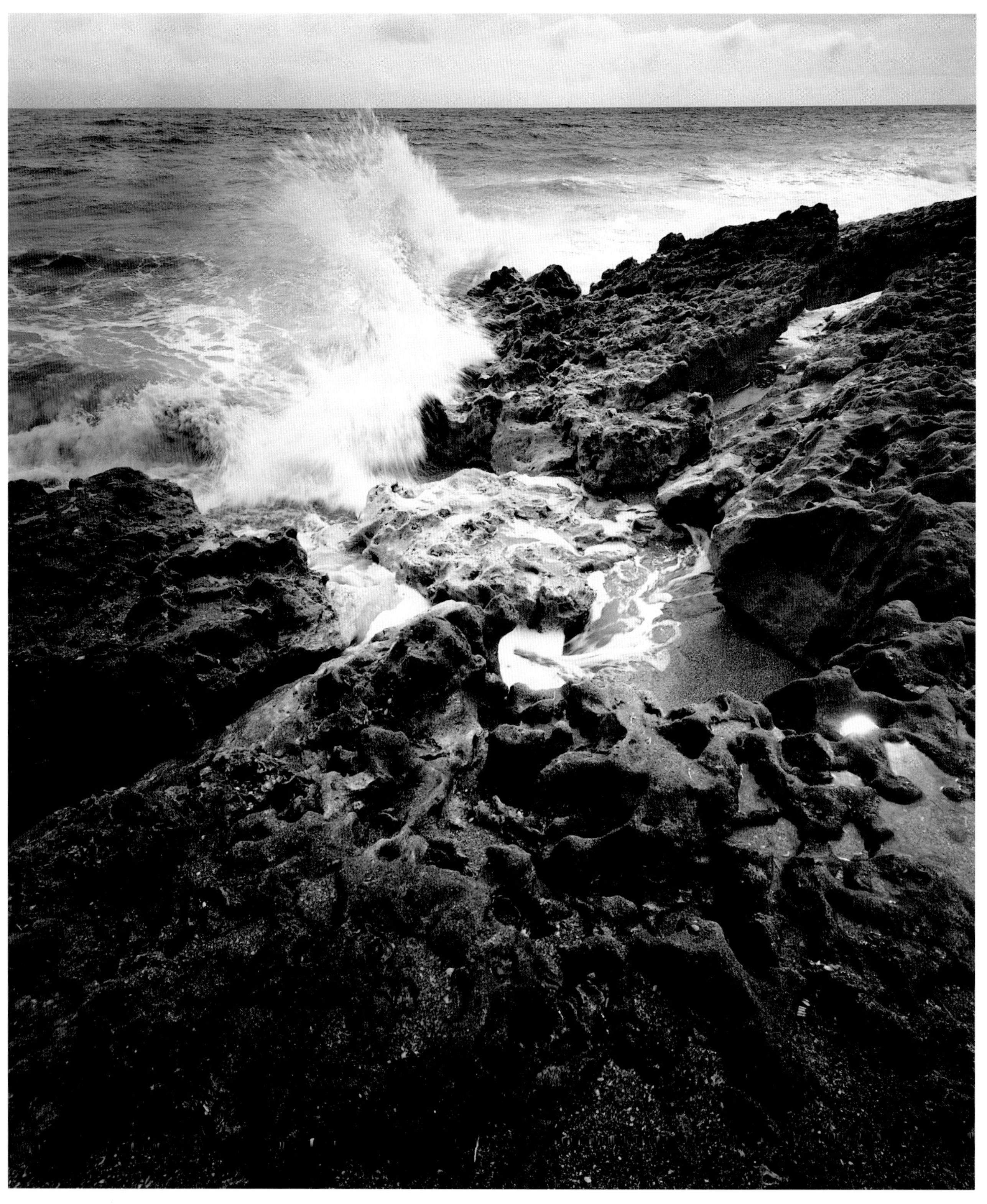

Blowing Rocks #10
Plate 5

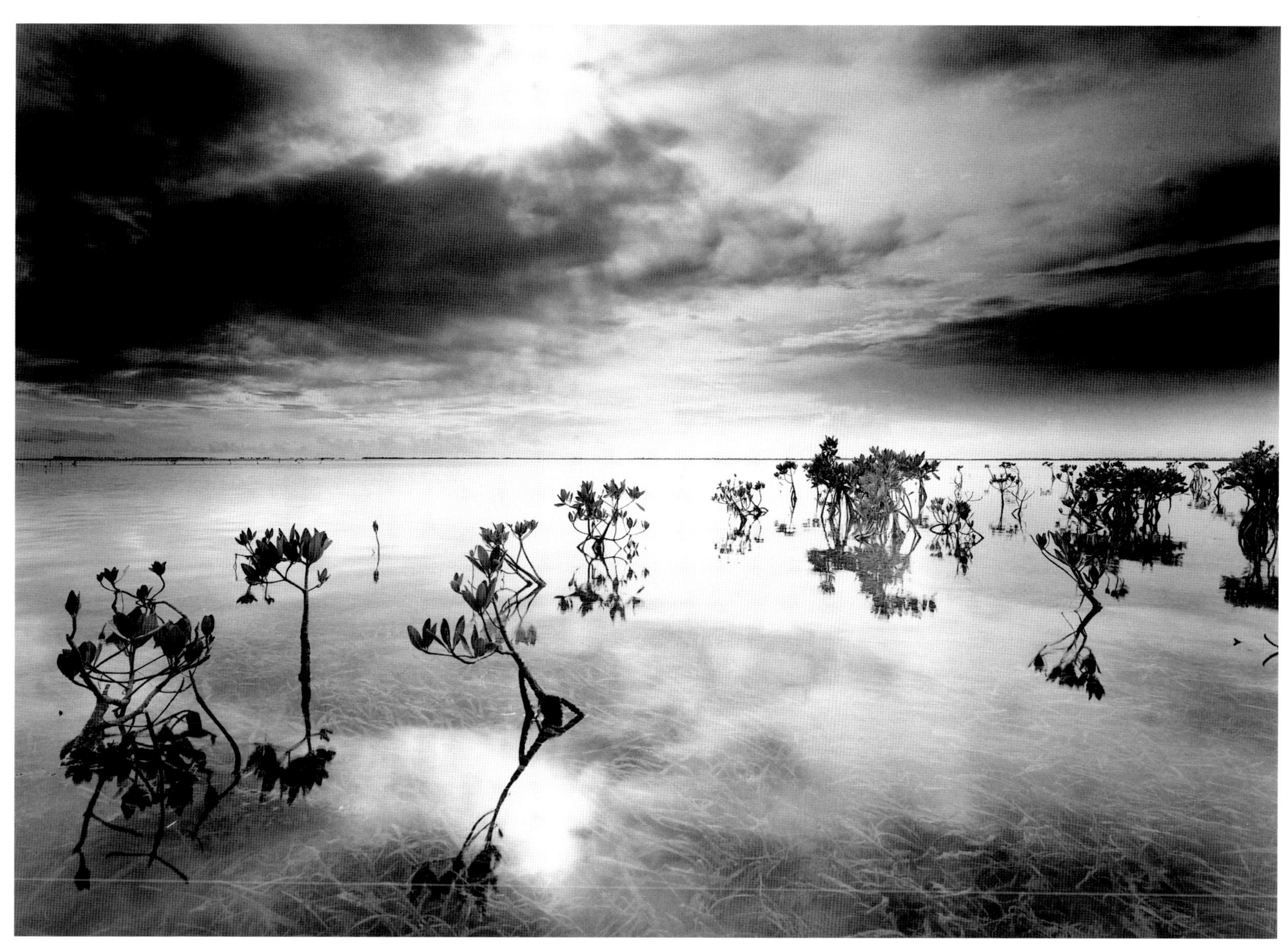

Linderman Key
Plate 6

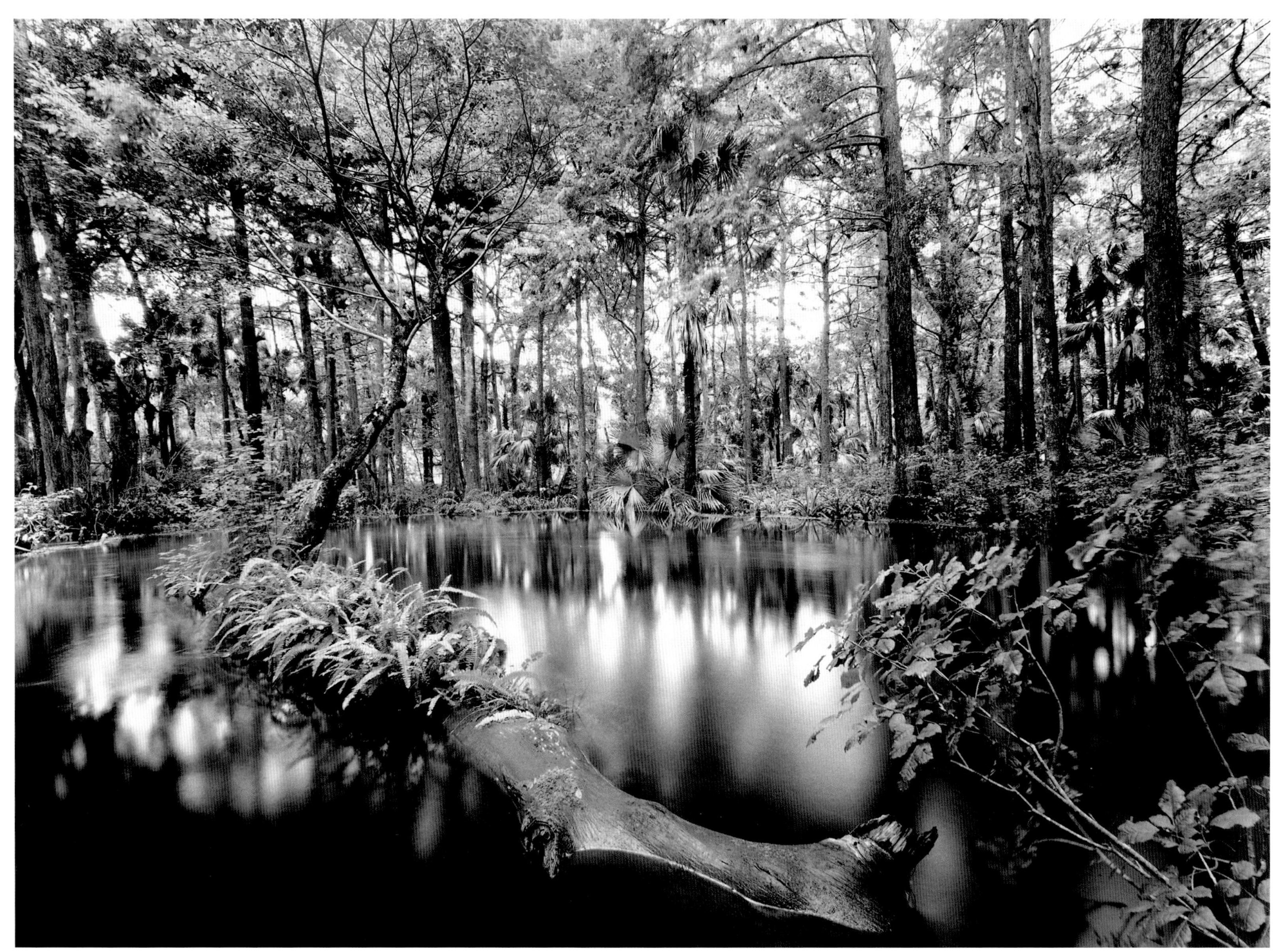

Loxahatchee River #1
Plate 7

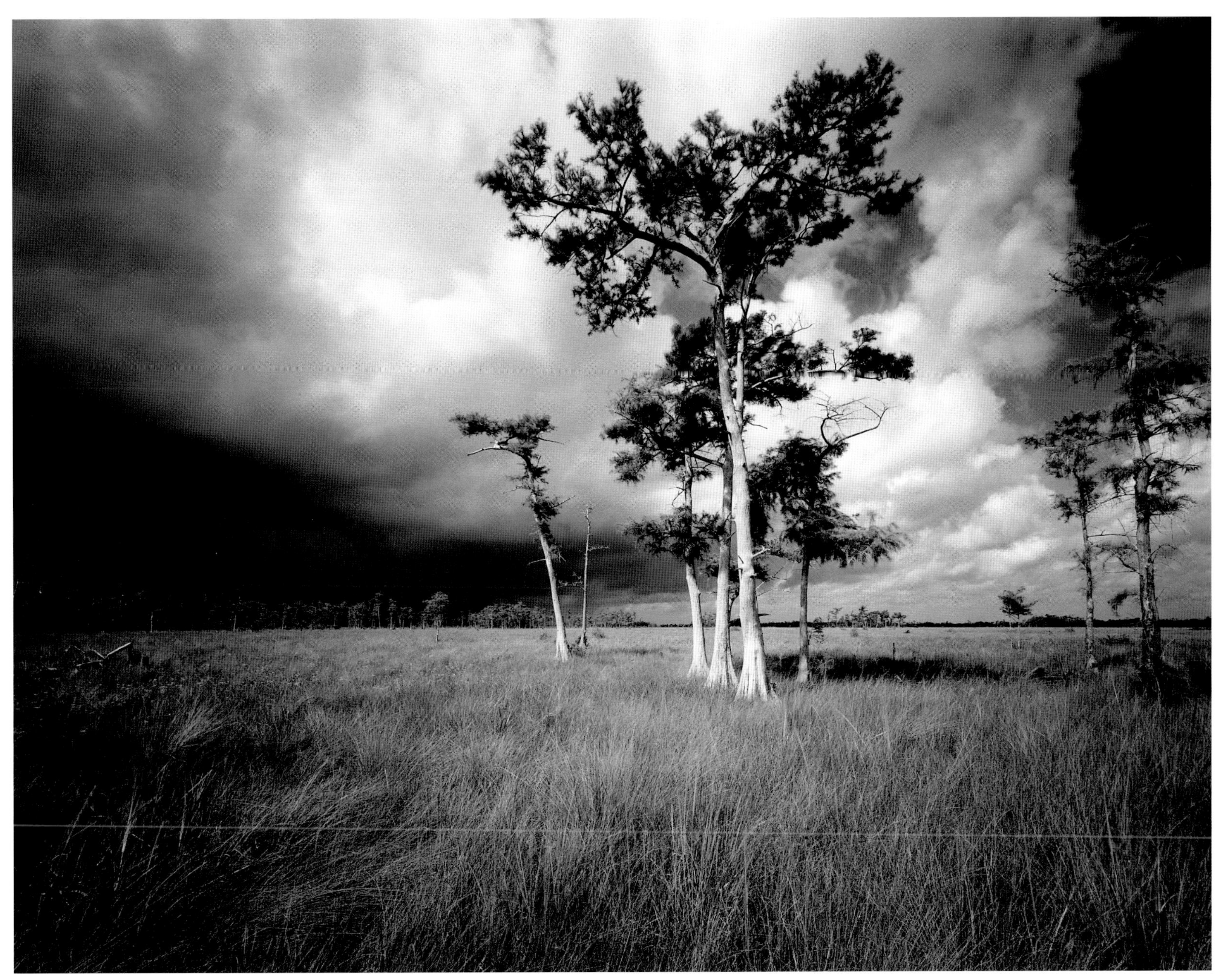

Tamiami Trail #2
Plate 8

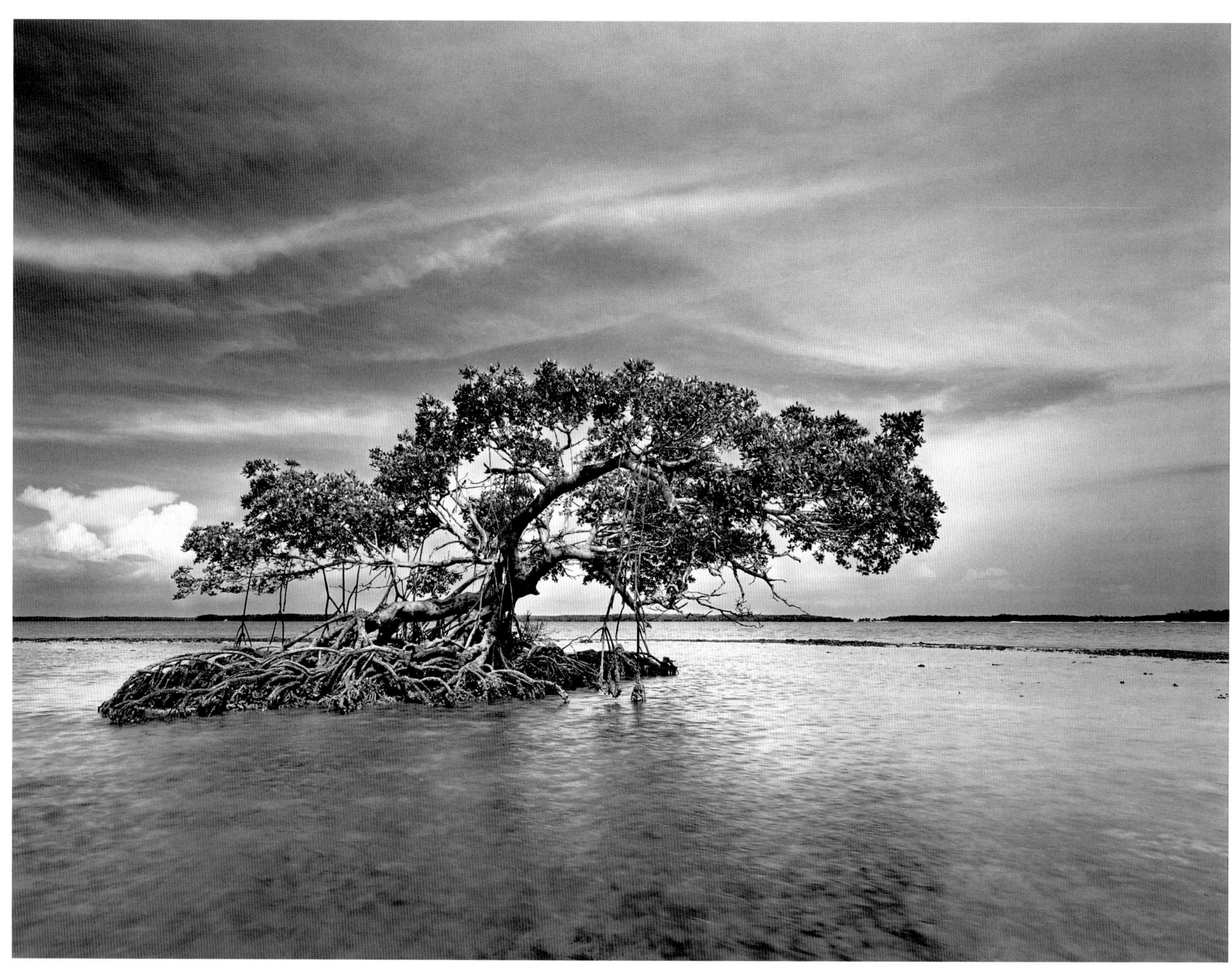

Indian Key Pass #6
Plate 9

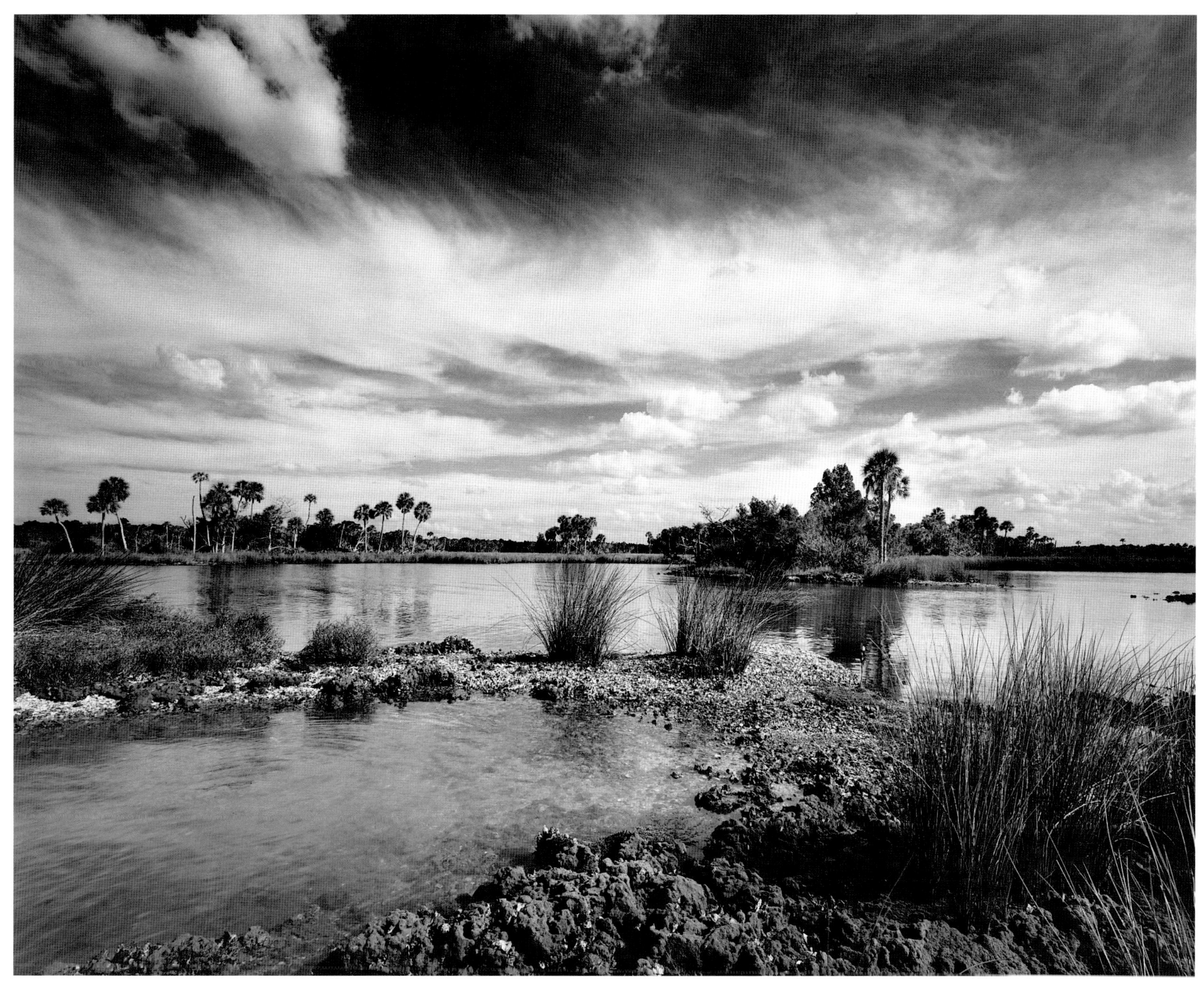

Homossassas Springs
Plate 10

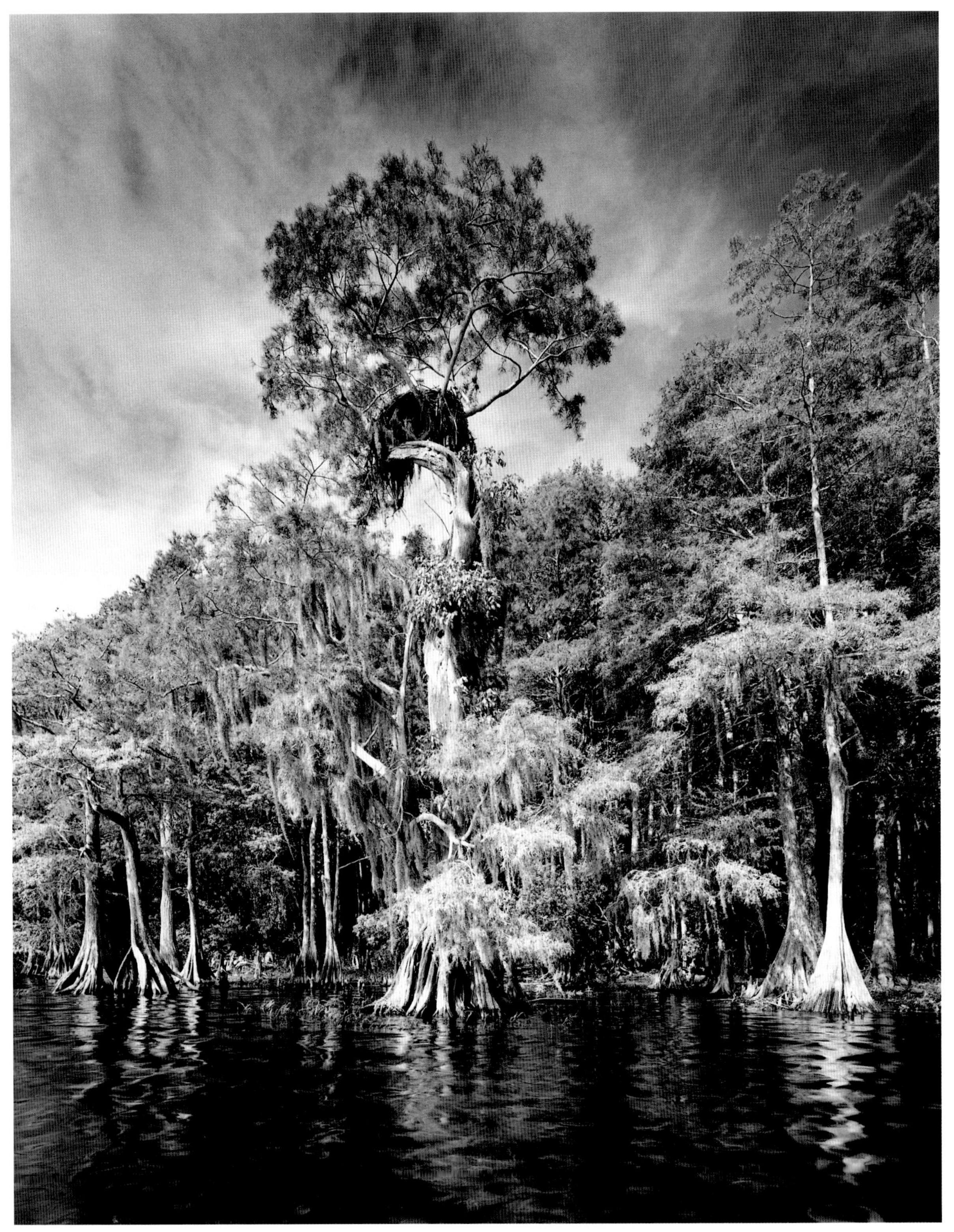

Osprey Nest
Plate 11

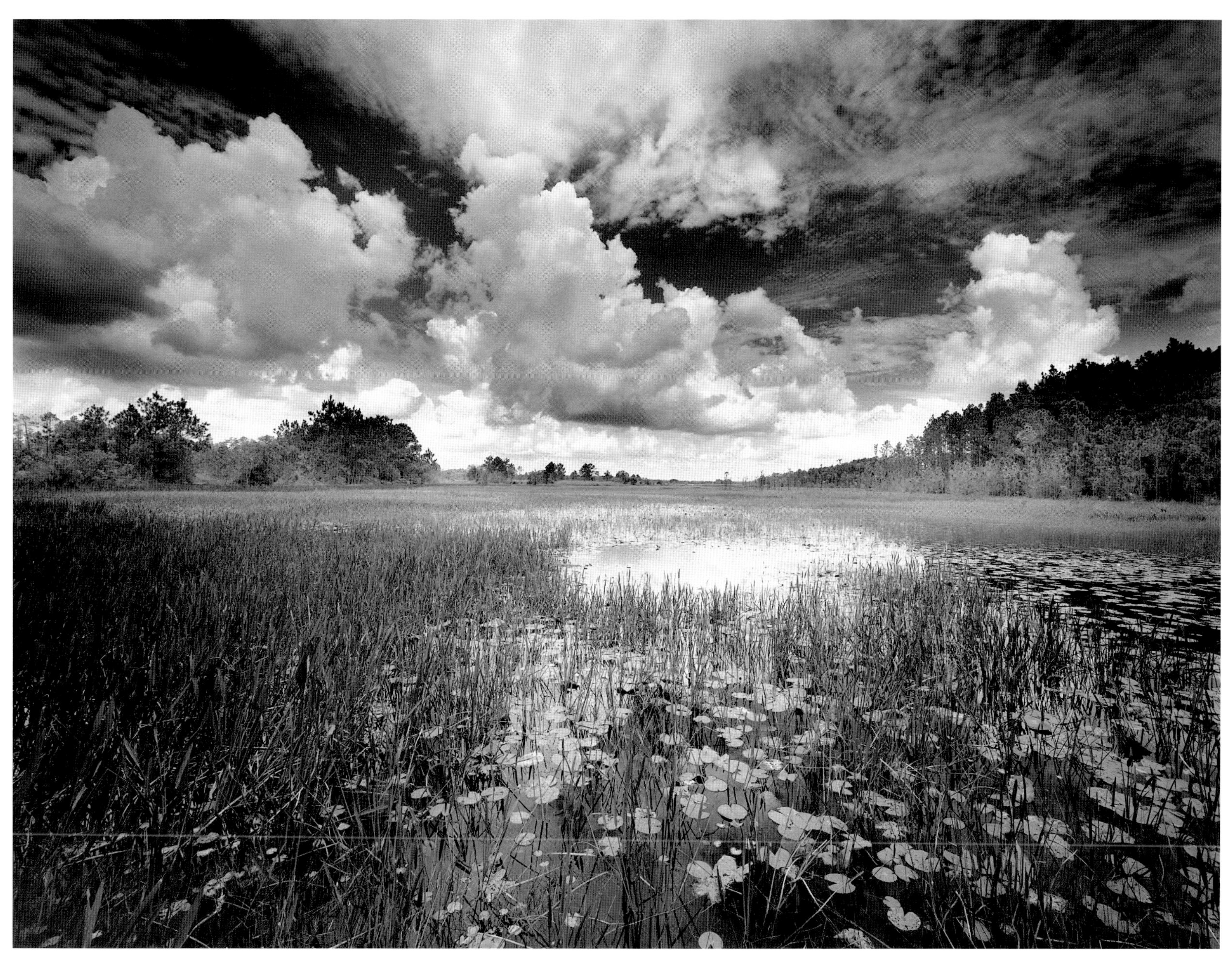

Grand Swamp
Plate 12

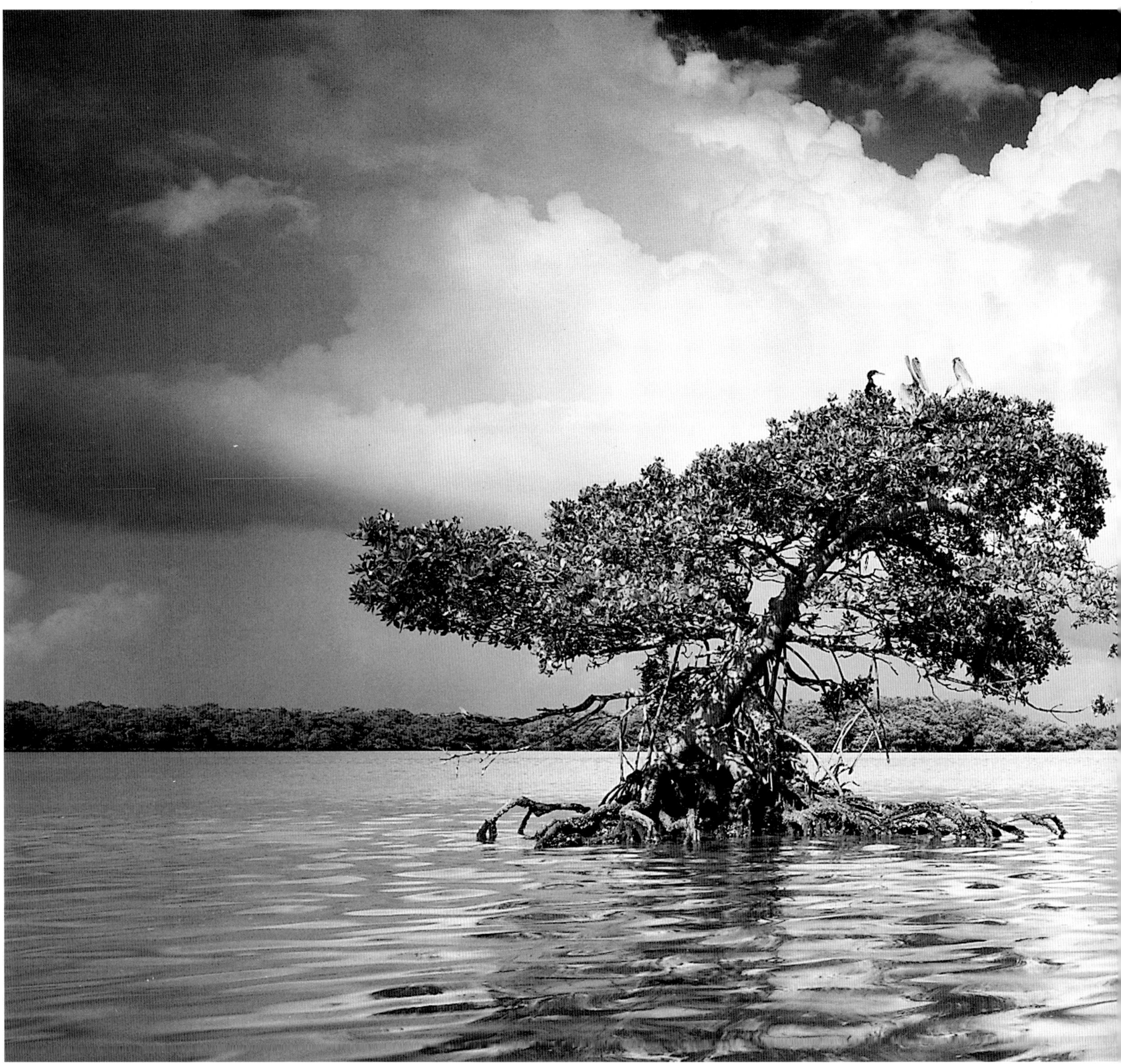

Gaskin #5   Plate 13

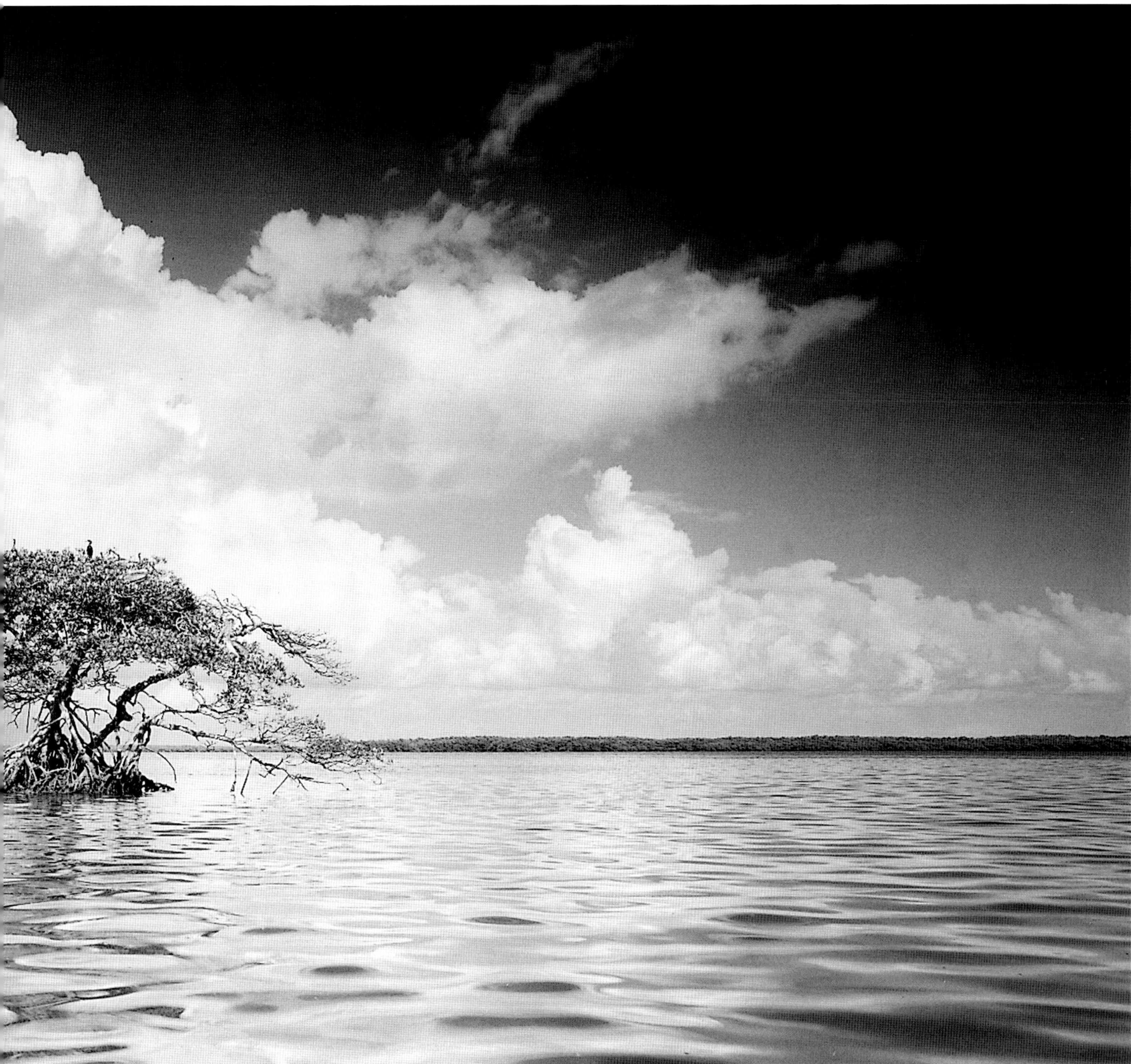

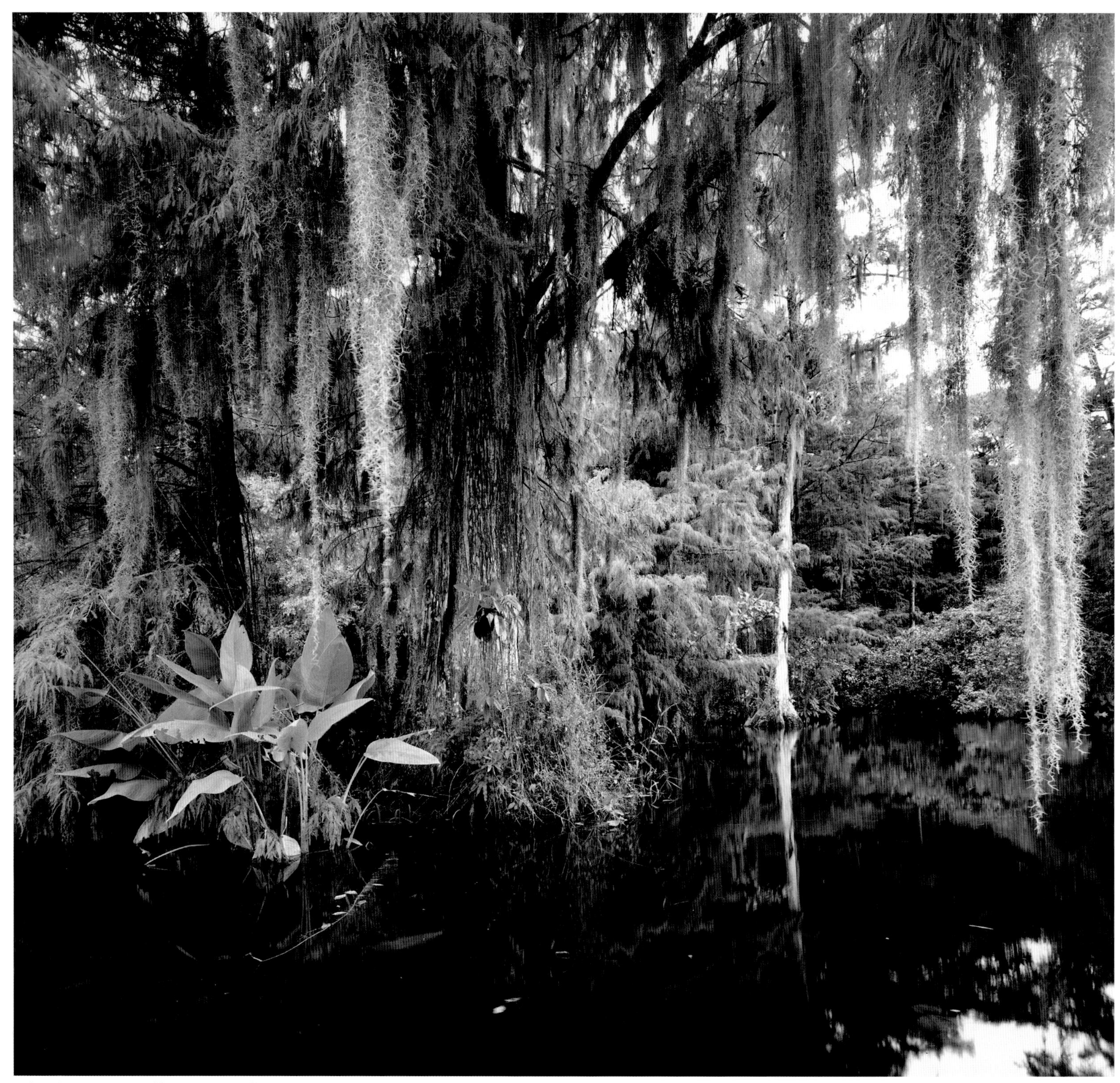

Big Cypress Gallery #2   Plate 14

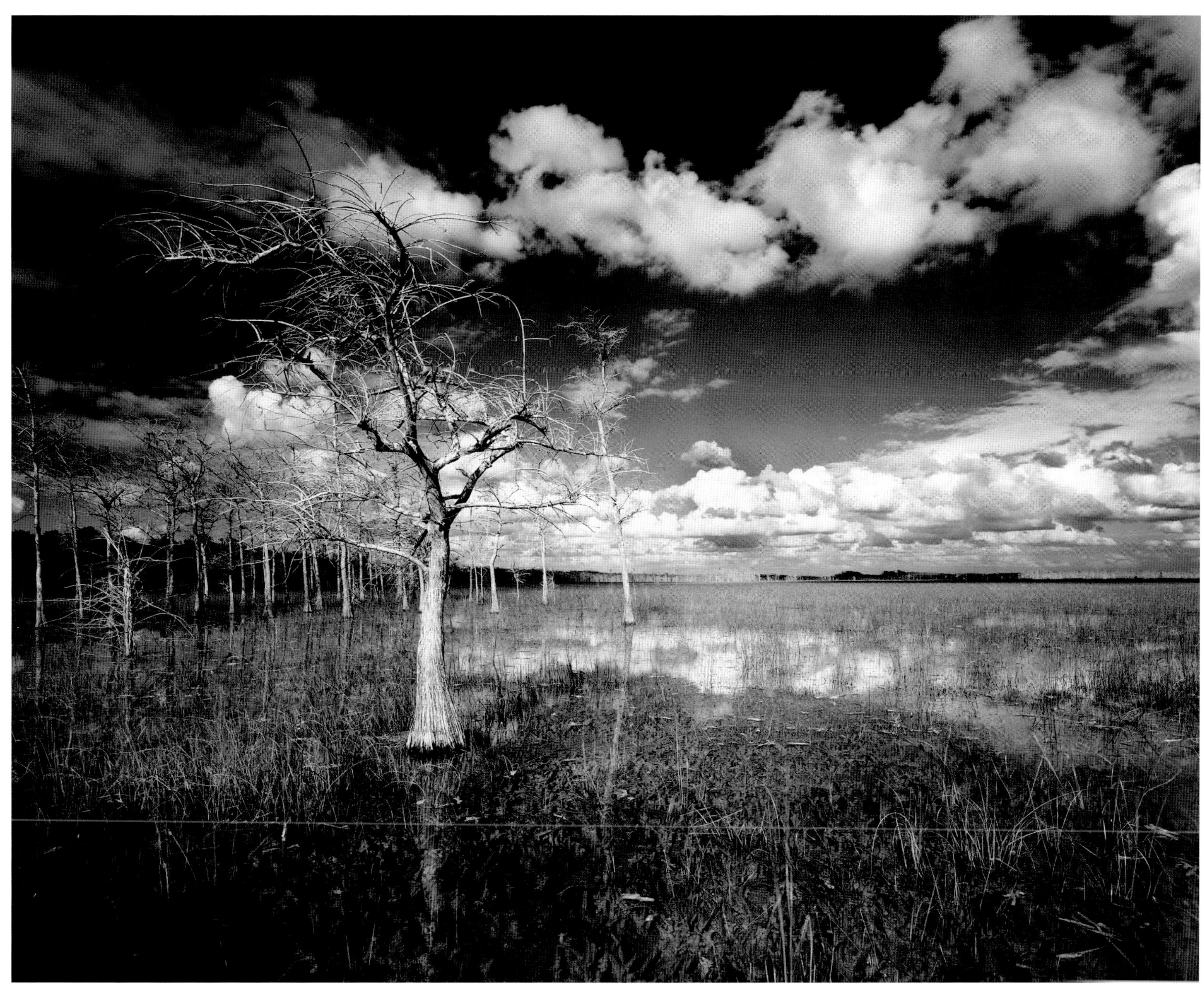

Gannet Strand
Plate 15

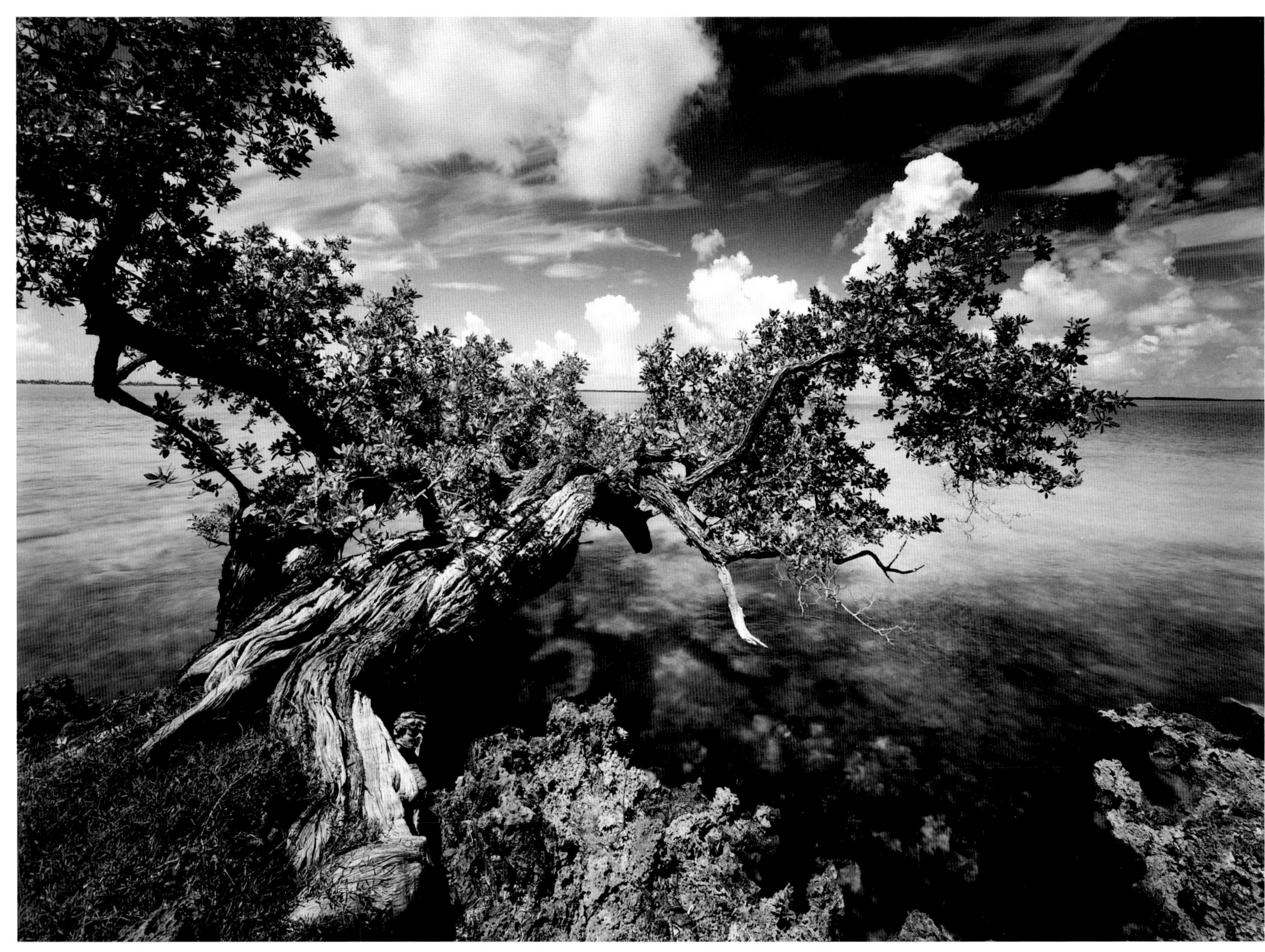

Key Largo Buttonwood #1
Plate 16

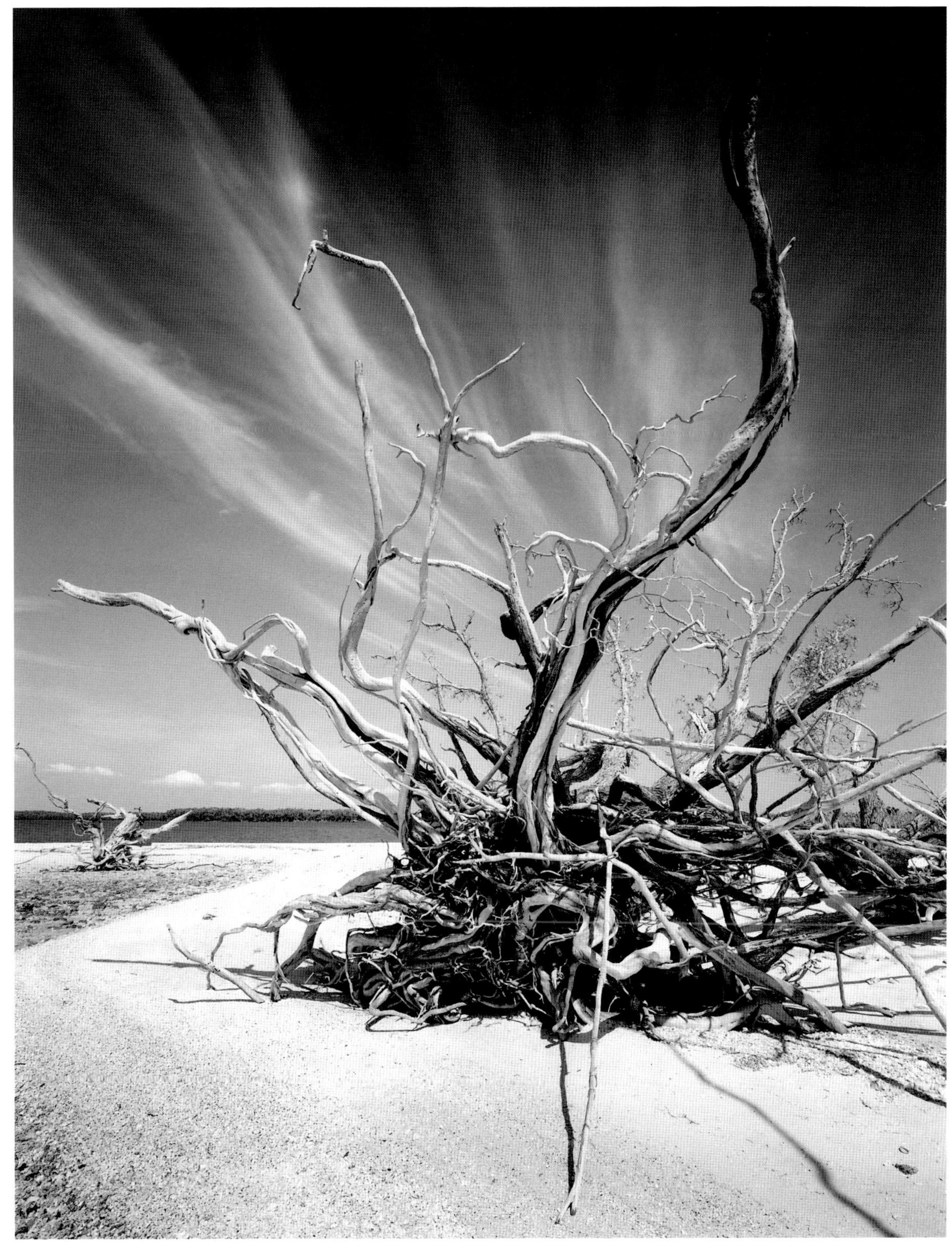

Indian Key #5
Plate 17

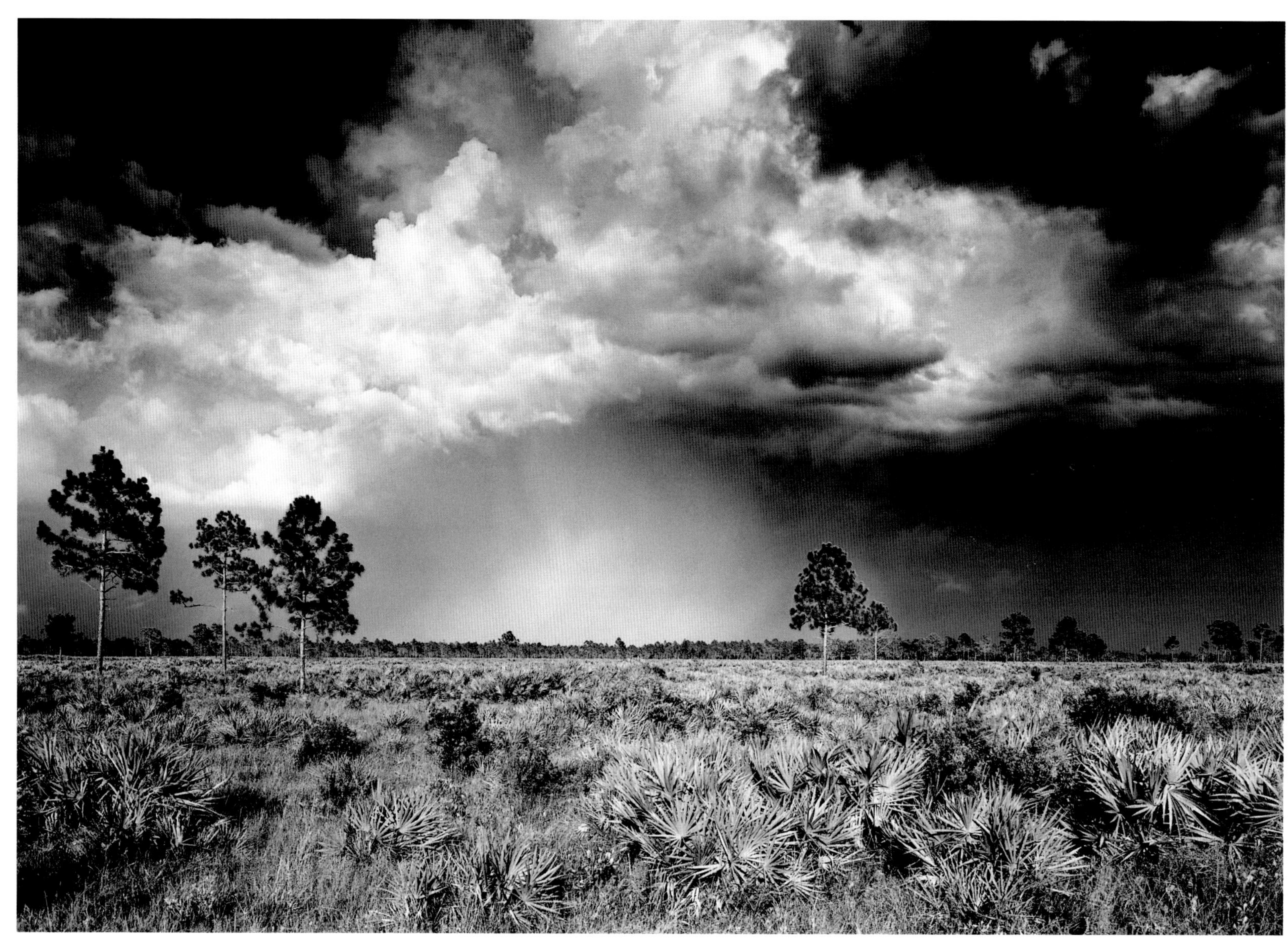

Trout Creek
Plate 18

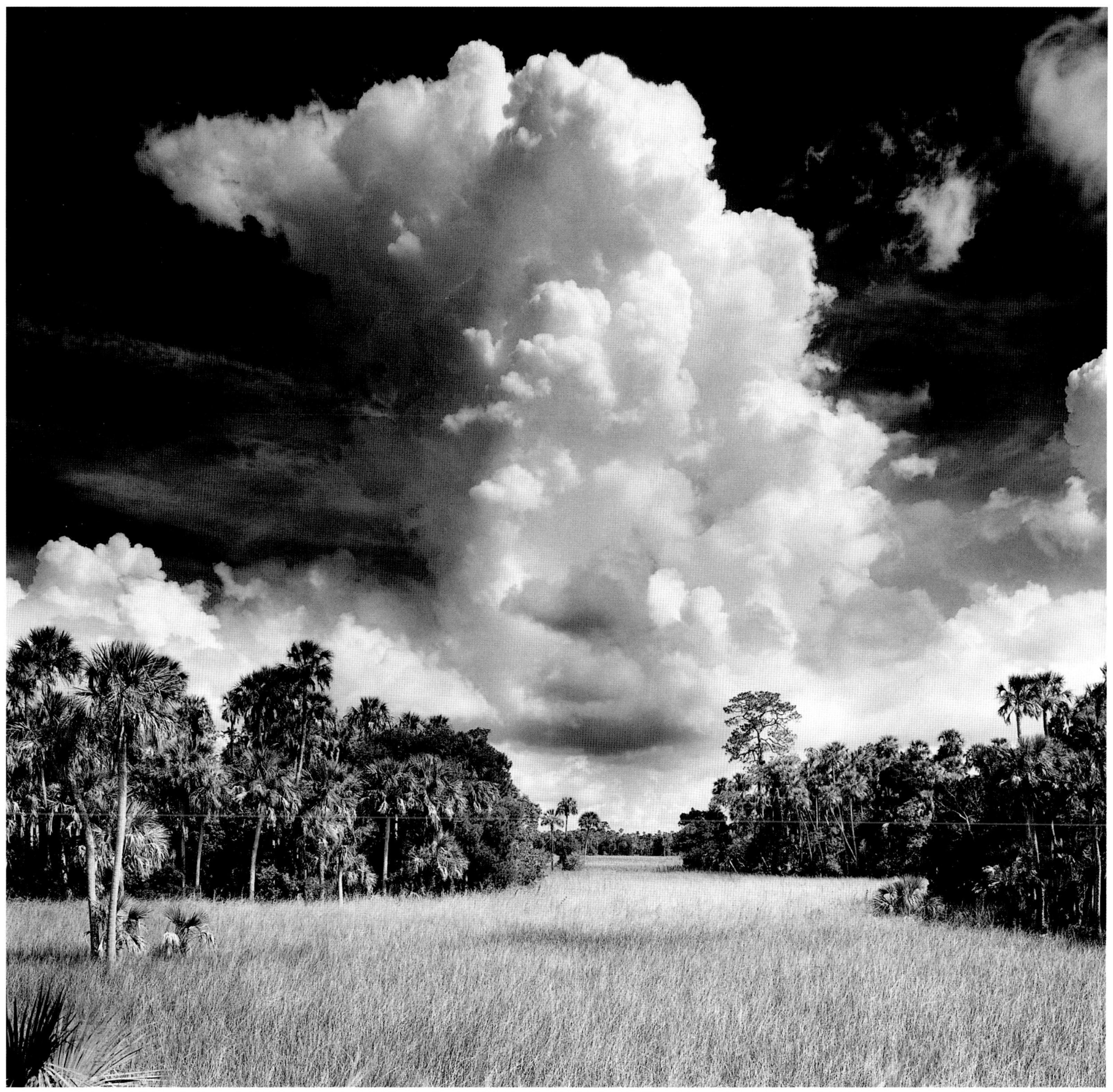

Crystal River   Plate 19

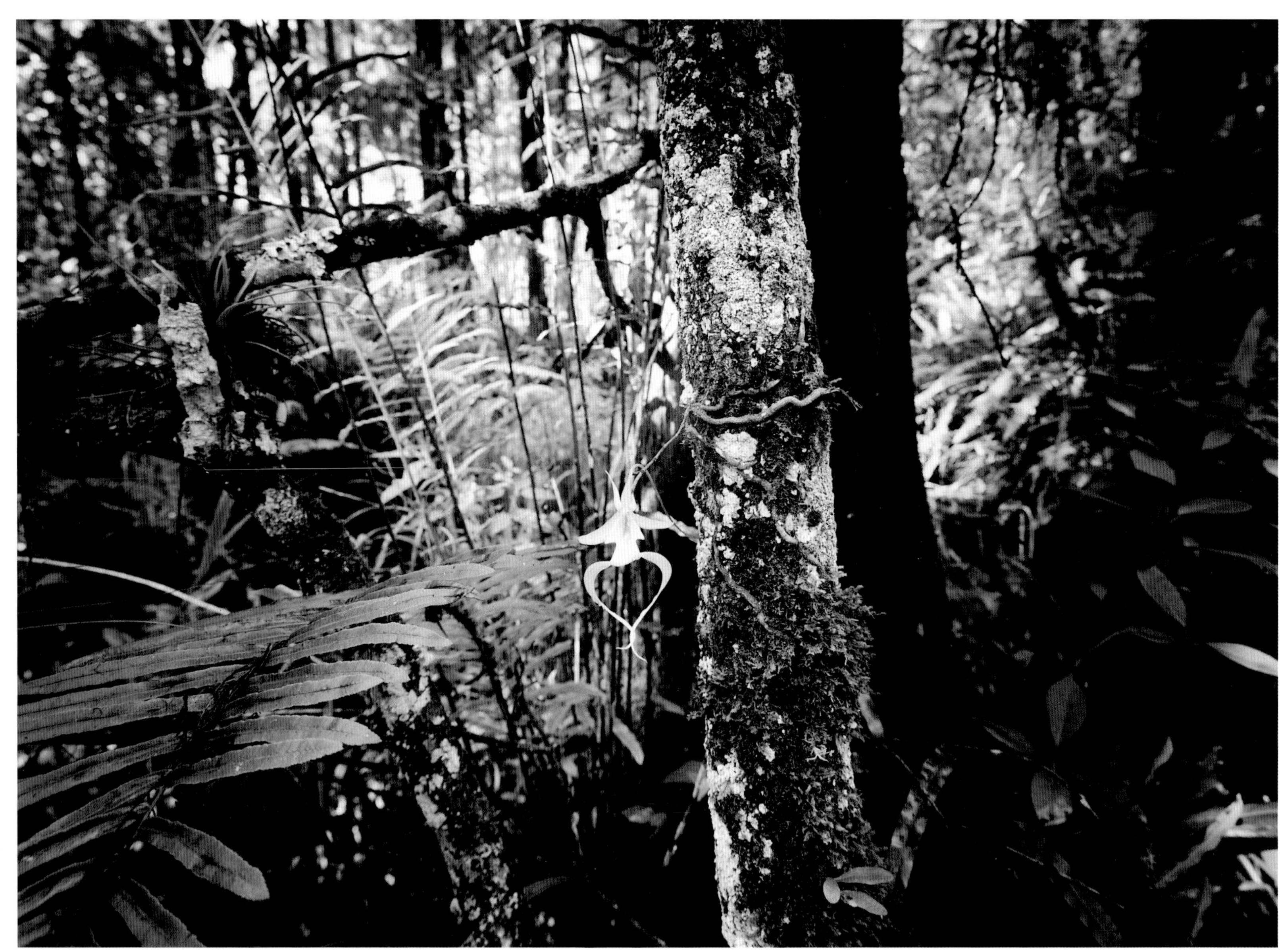

Ghost Orchid #2
Plate 20

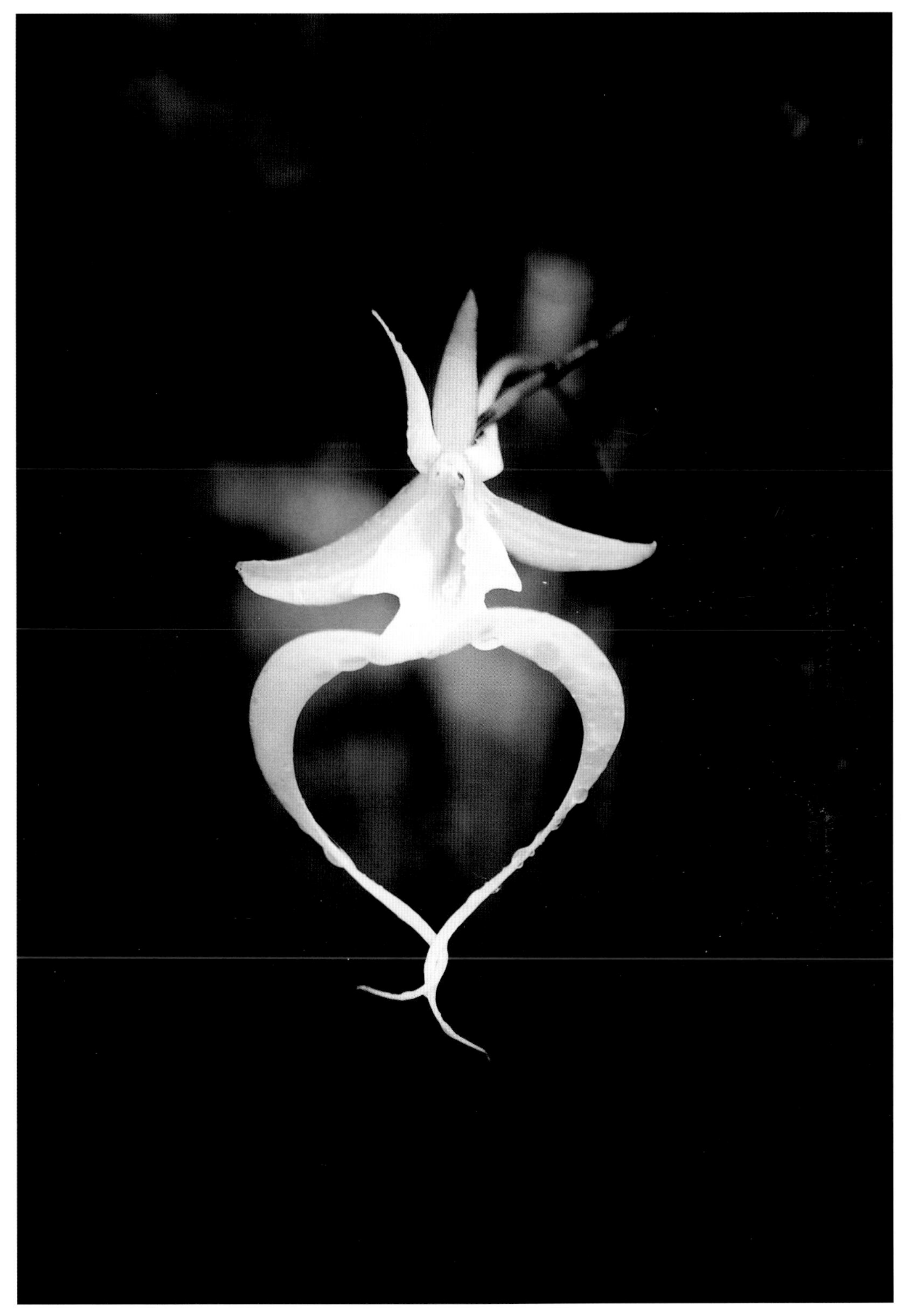

Ghost Orchid #1
Plate 21

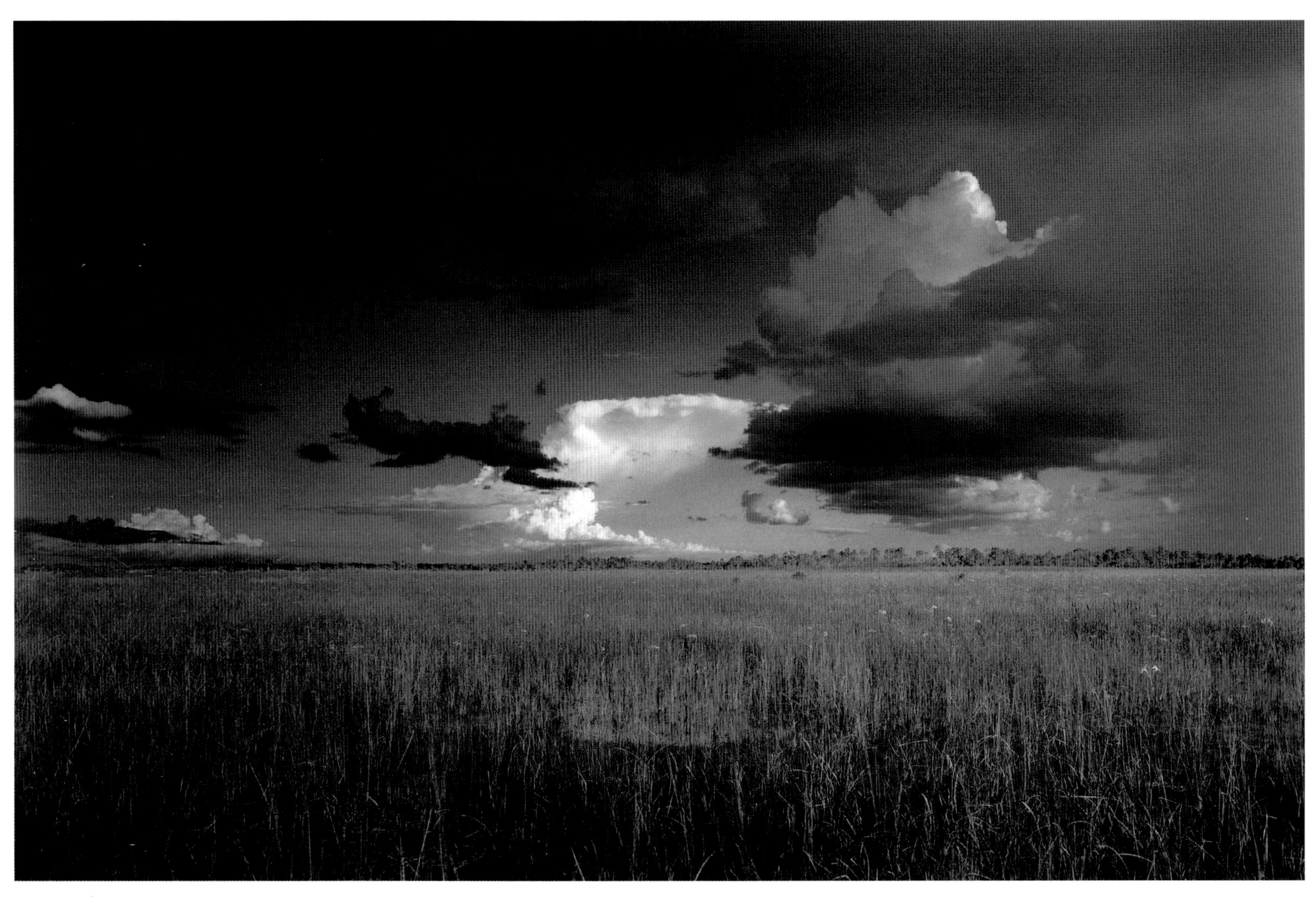

Wagon Wheel Road
Plate 22

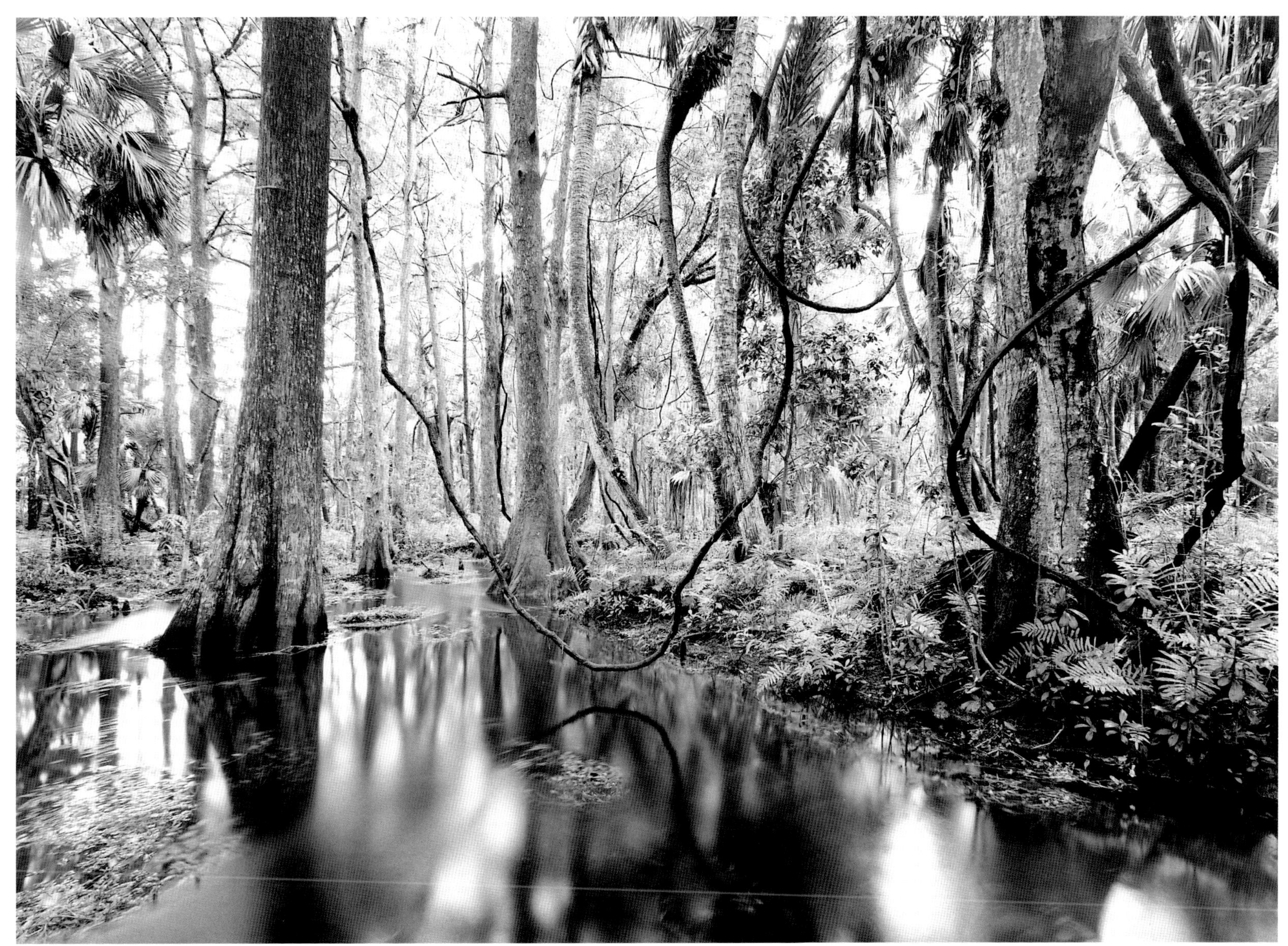

Loxahatchee River #7
Plate 23

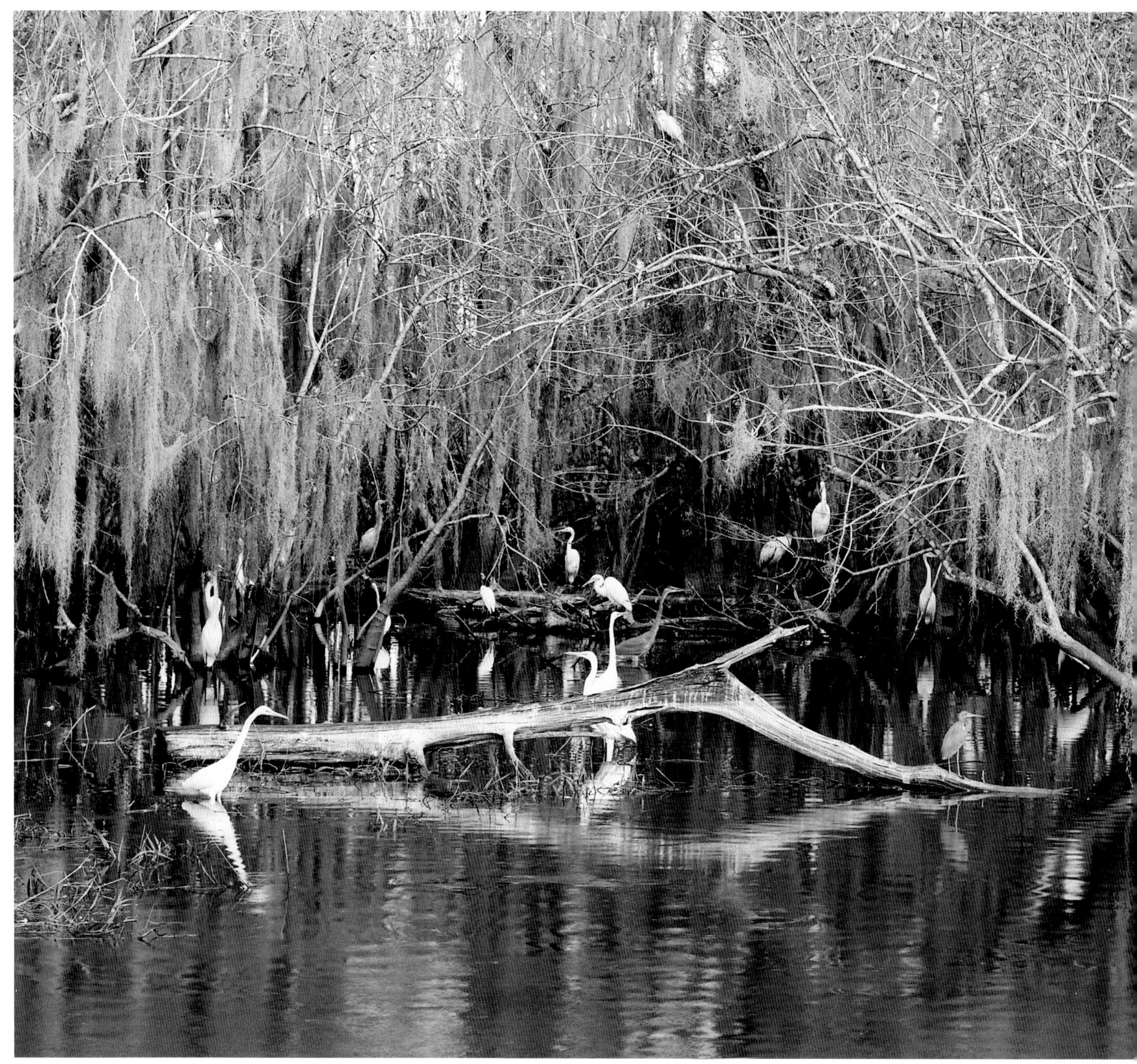

Skillet Strand Plate24

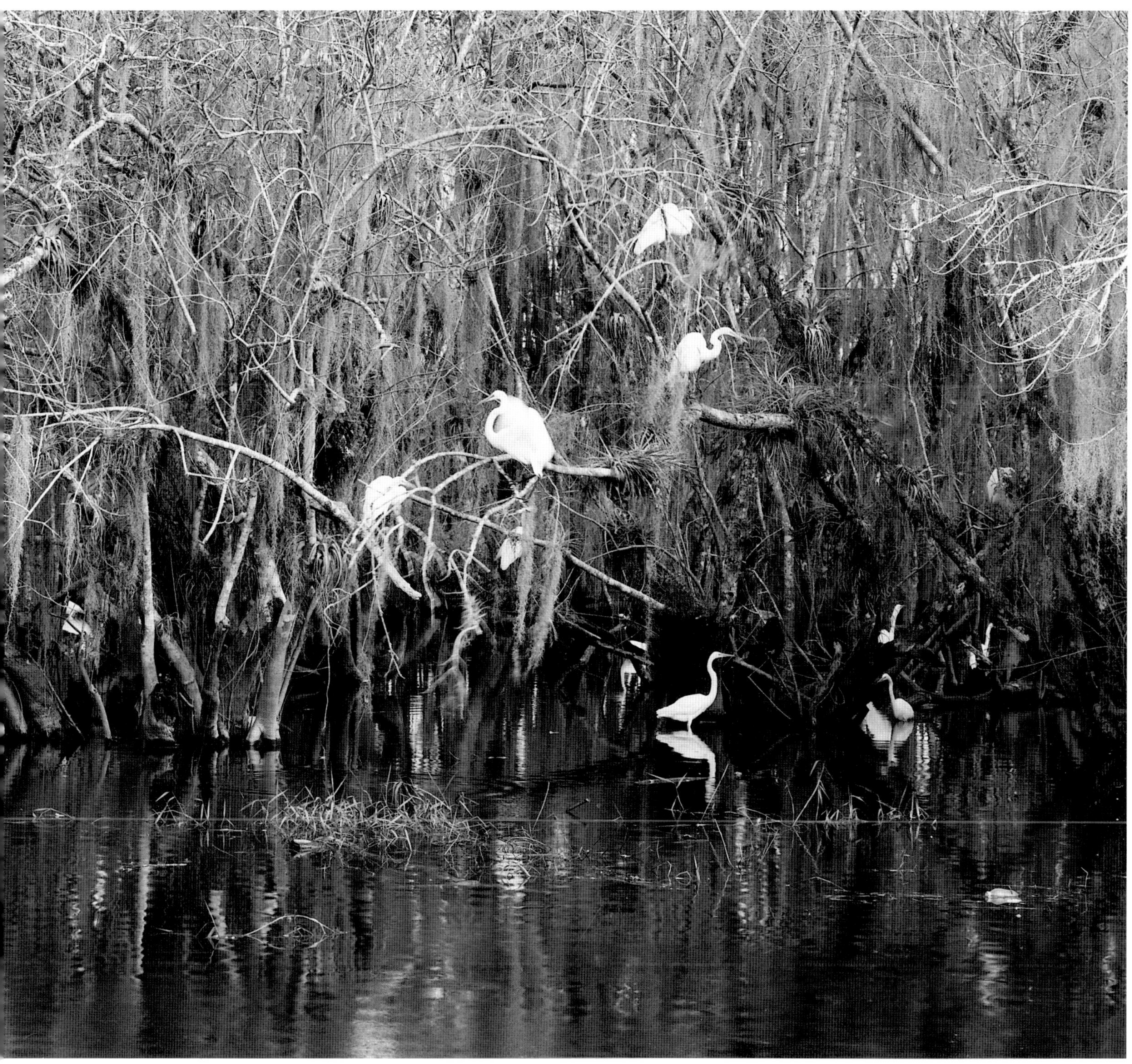

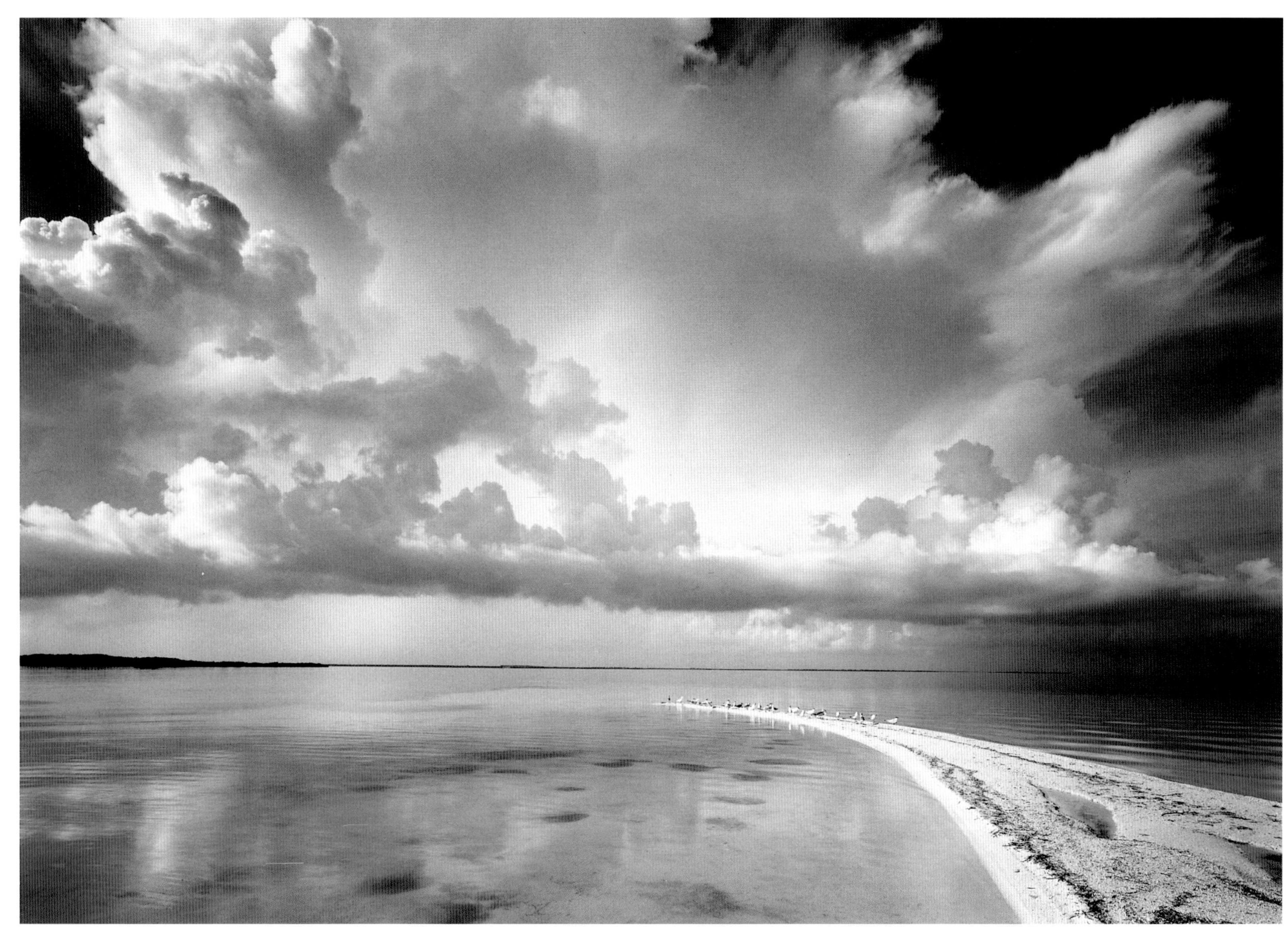

Little Butternut Key #1
Plate 25

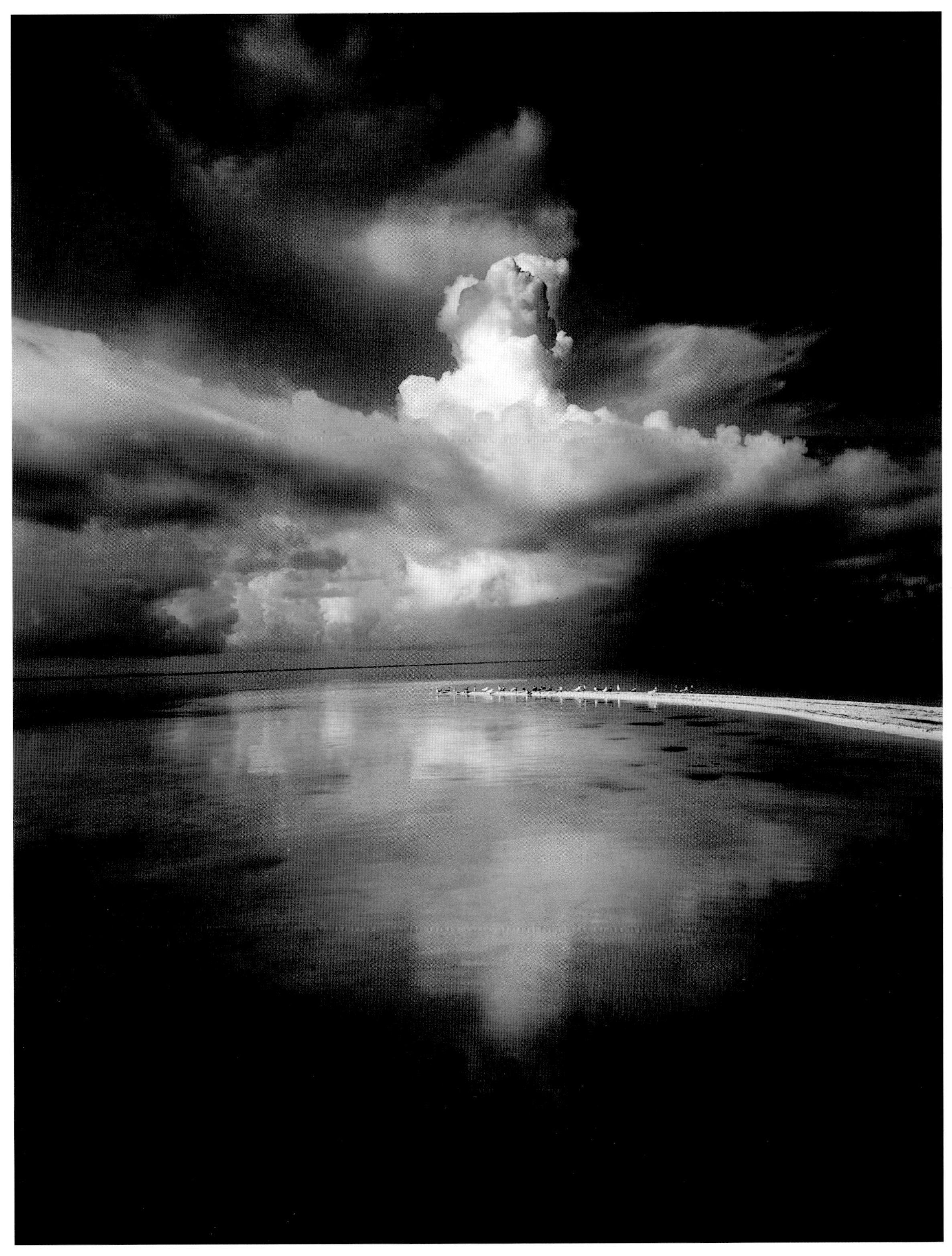

Little Butternut Key #2
Plate 26

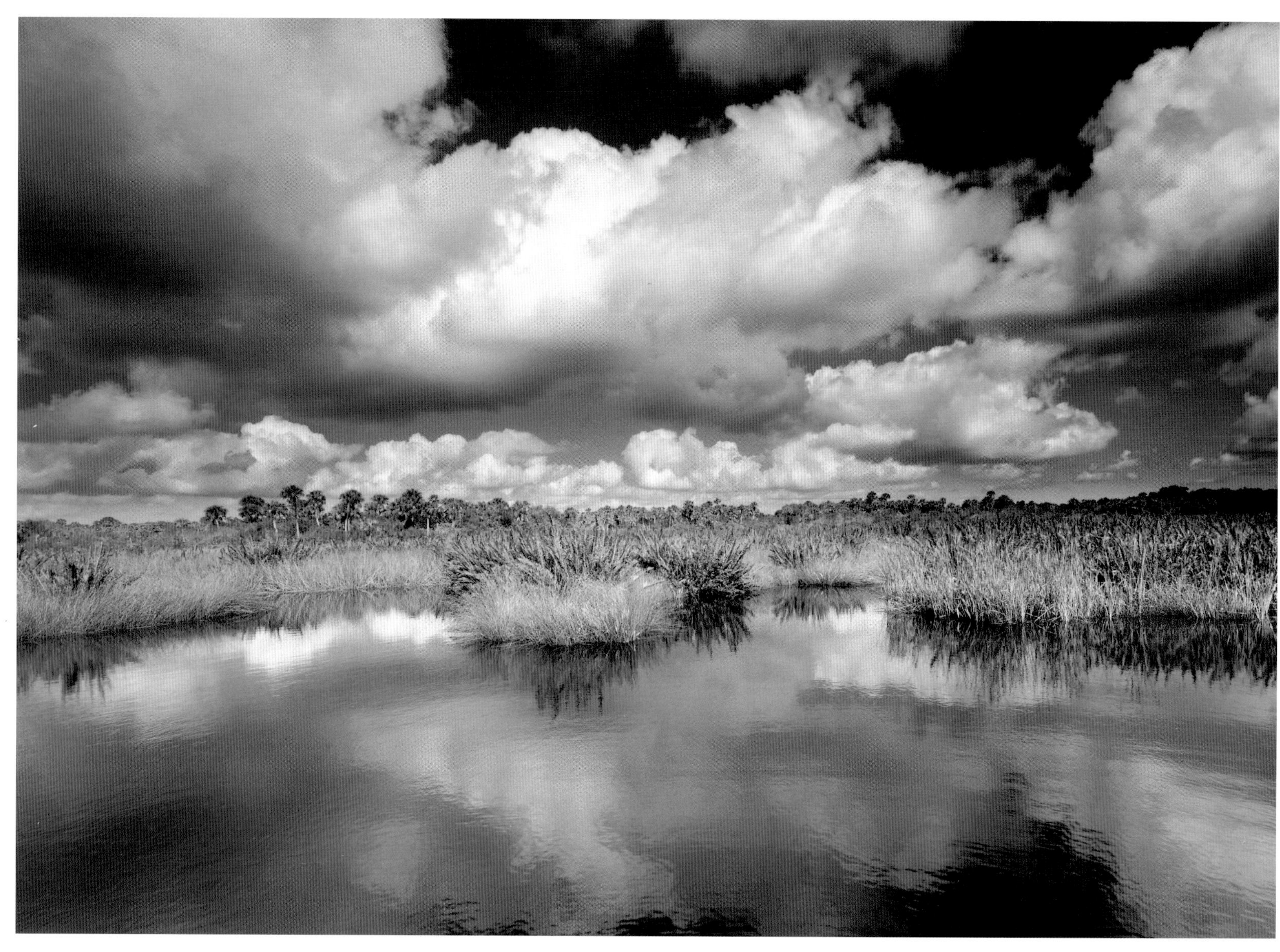

Myakka River
Plate 27

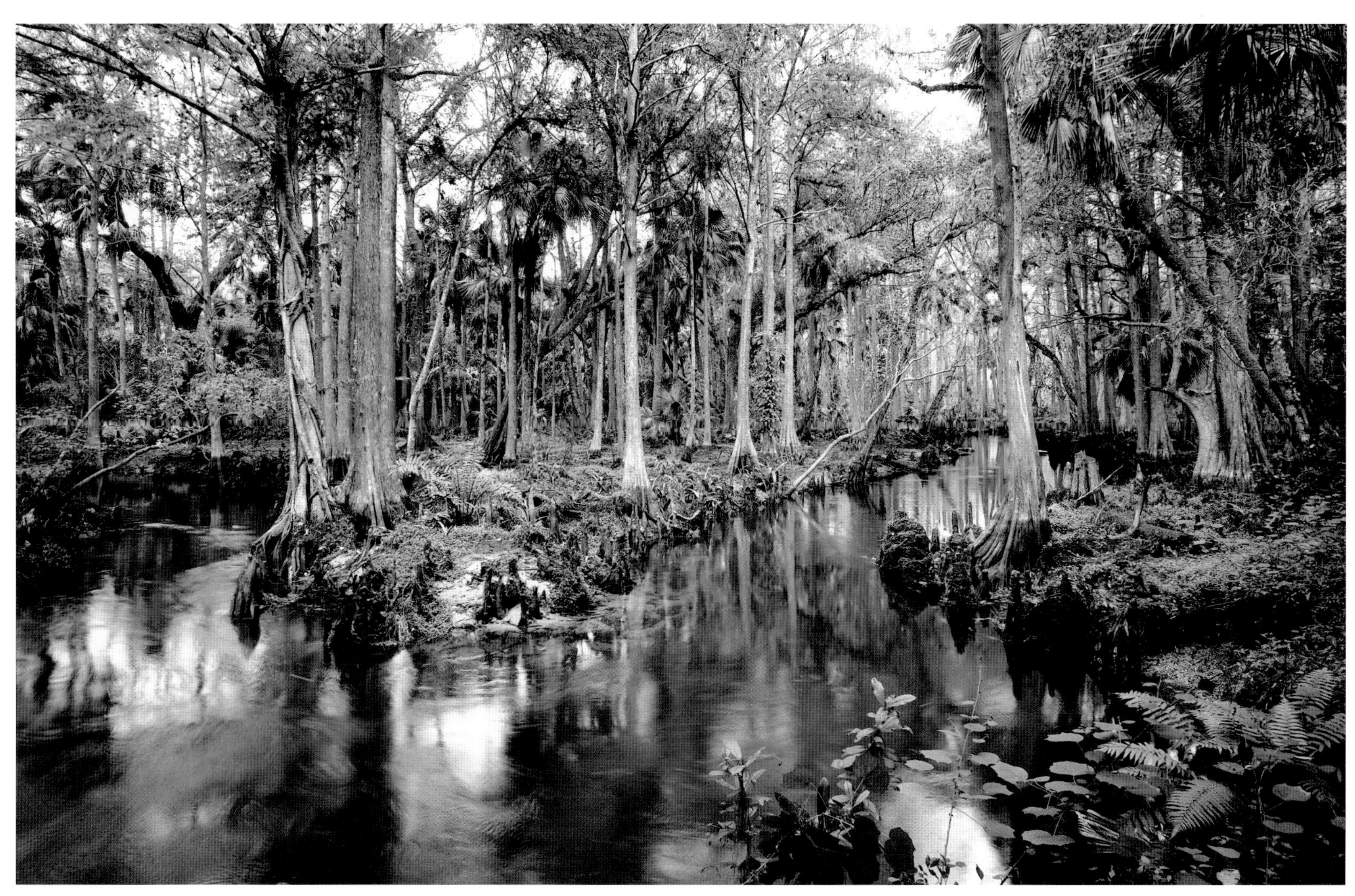

Loxahatchee River #9
Plate 28

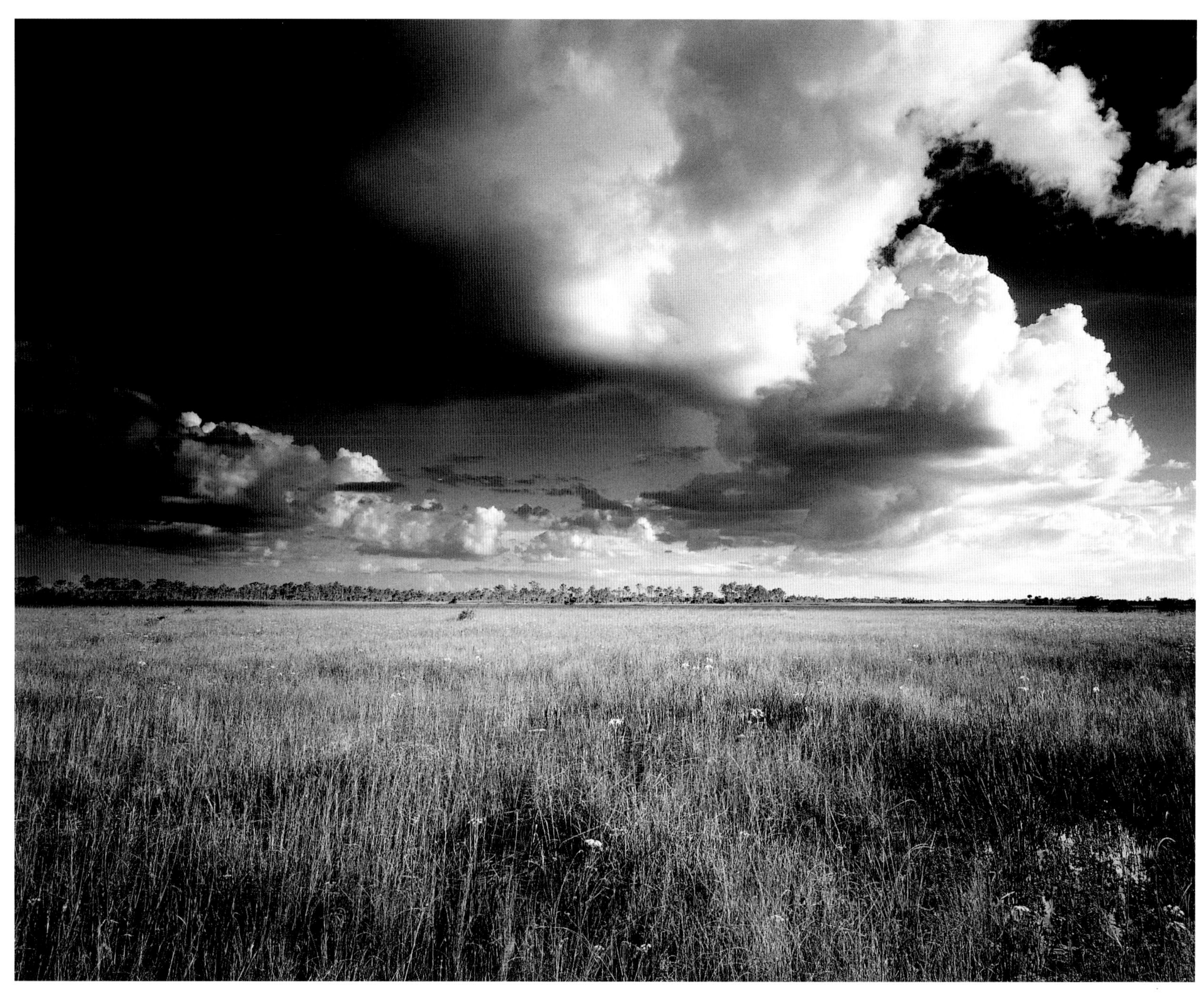

Everglades Restoration "Can Do"
Plate 29

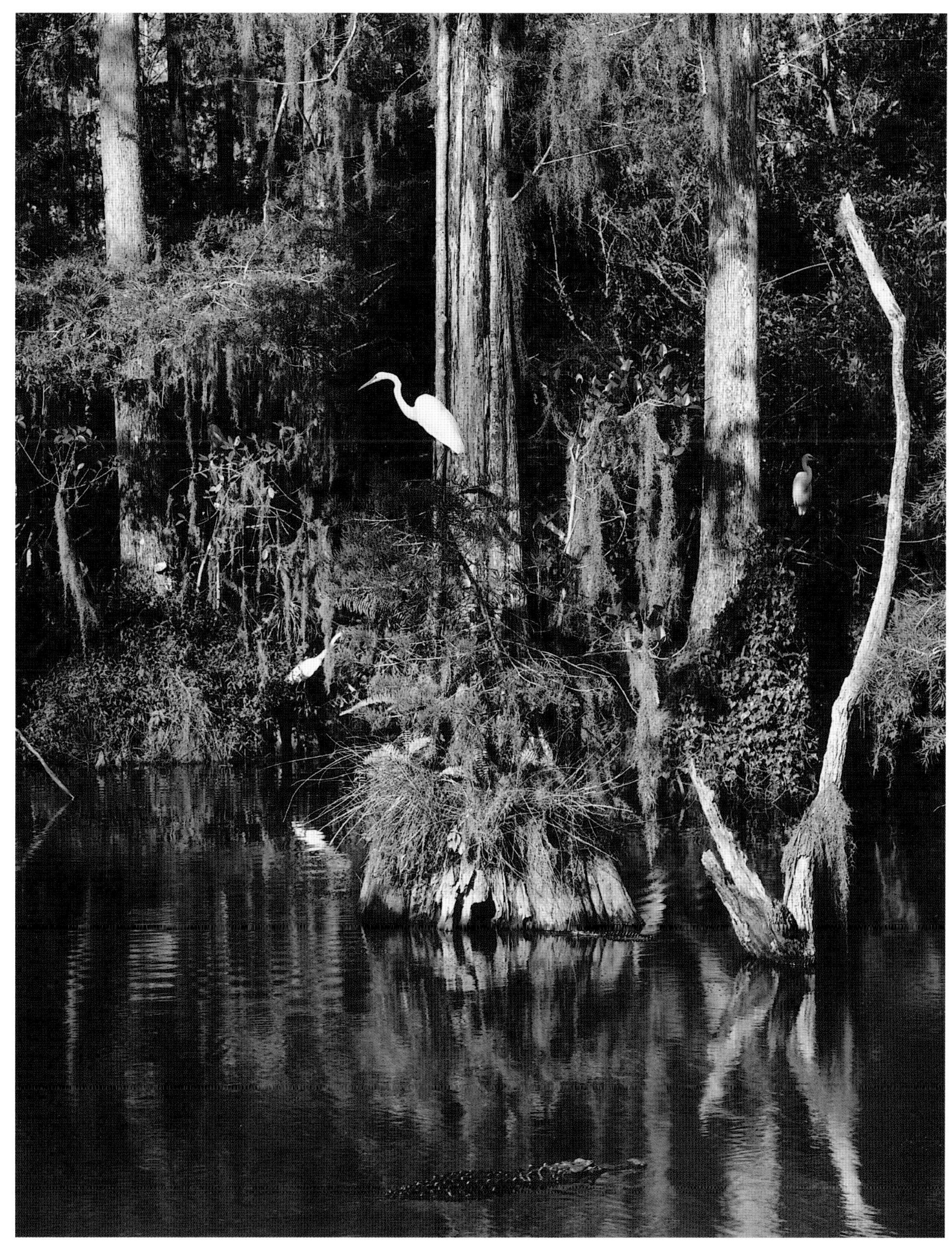

Big Cypress Gallery #14
Plate 30

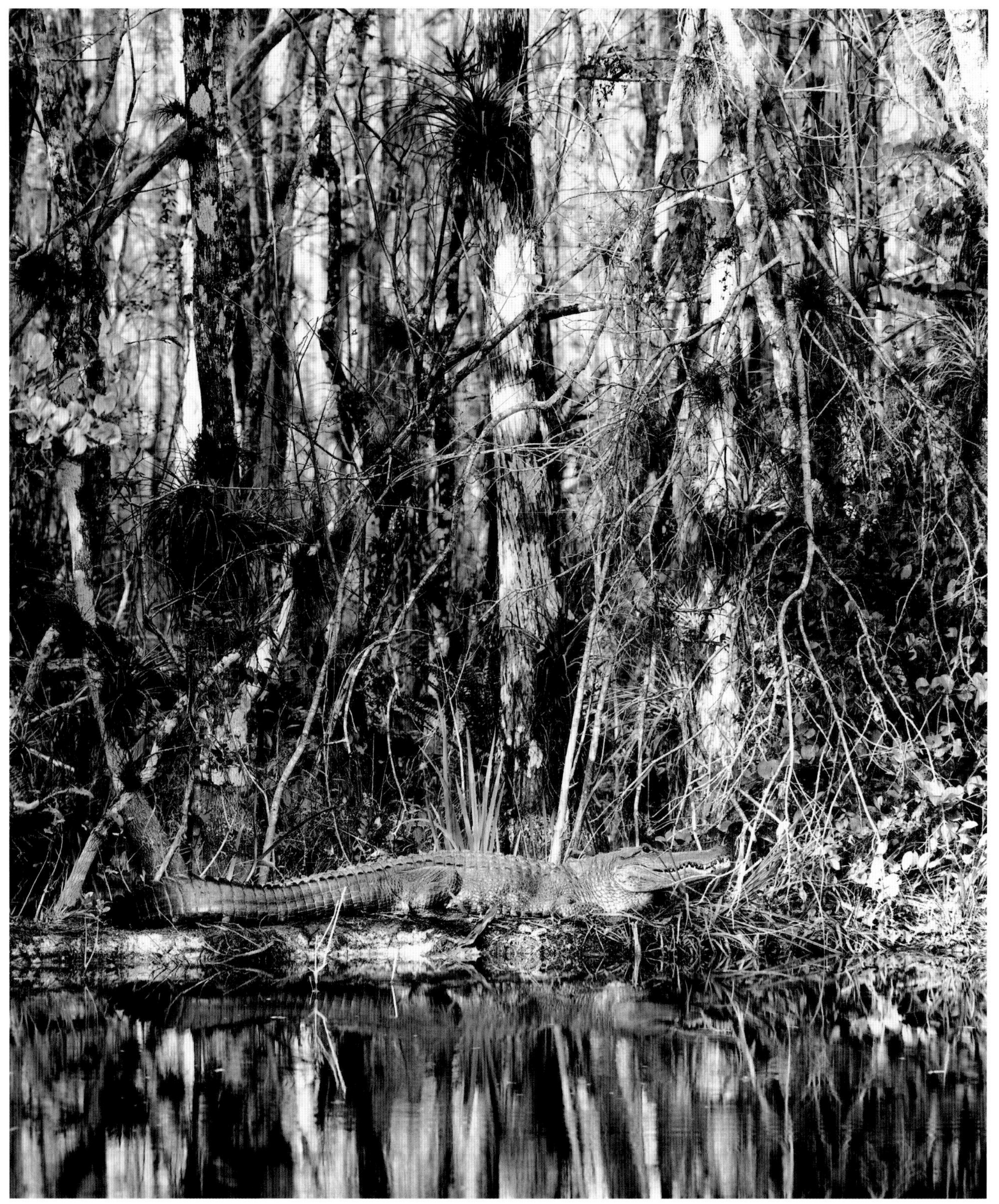

Loosescrew Gator
Plate 31

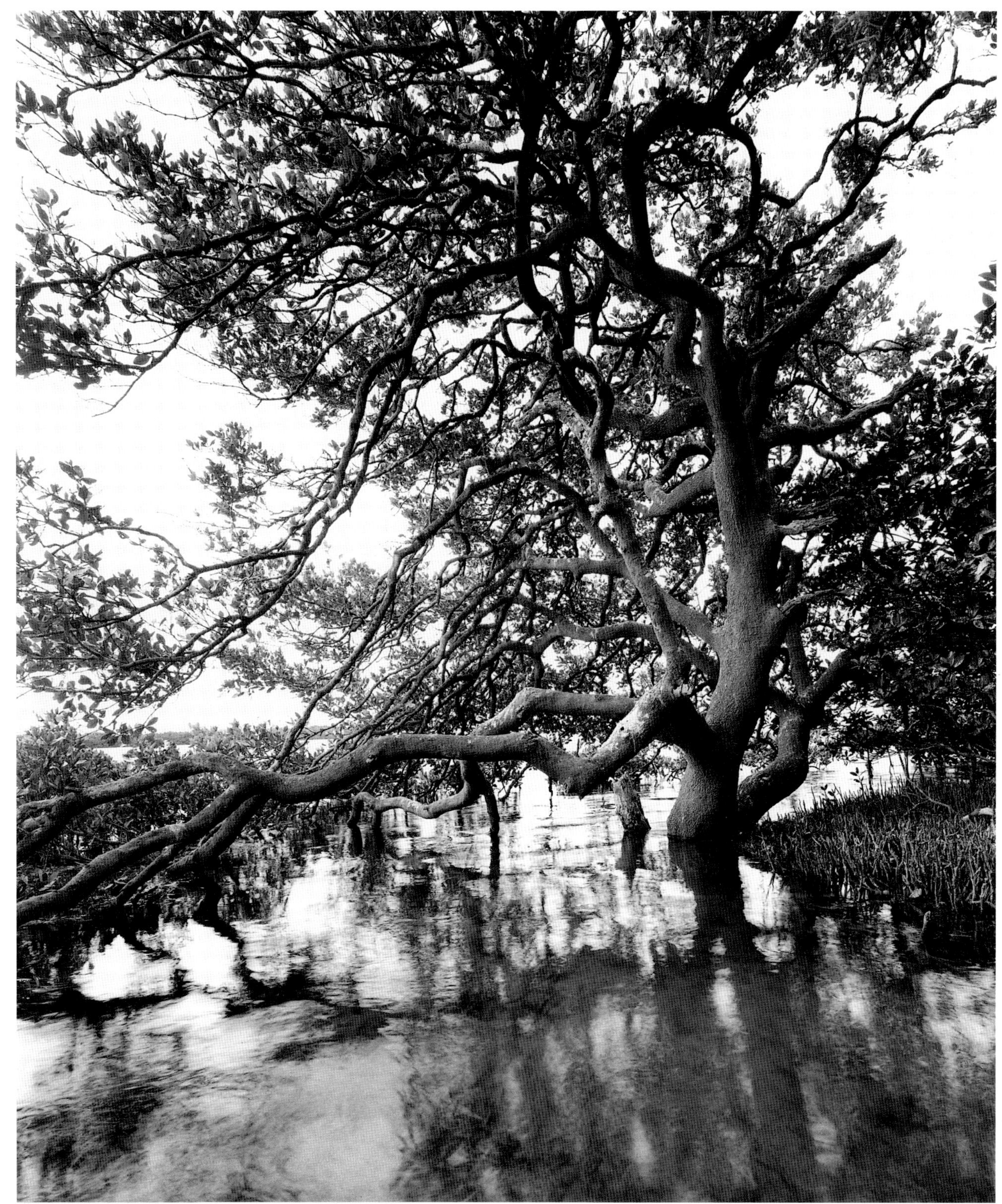

Black Mangrove
Plate 34

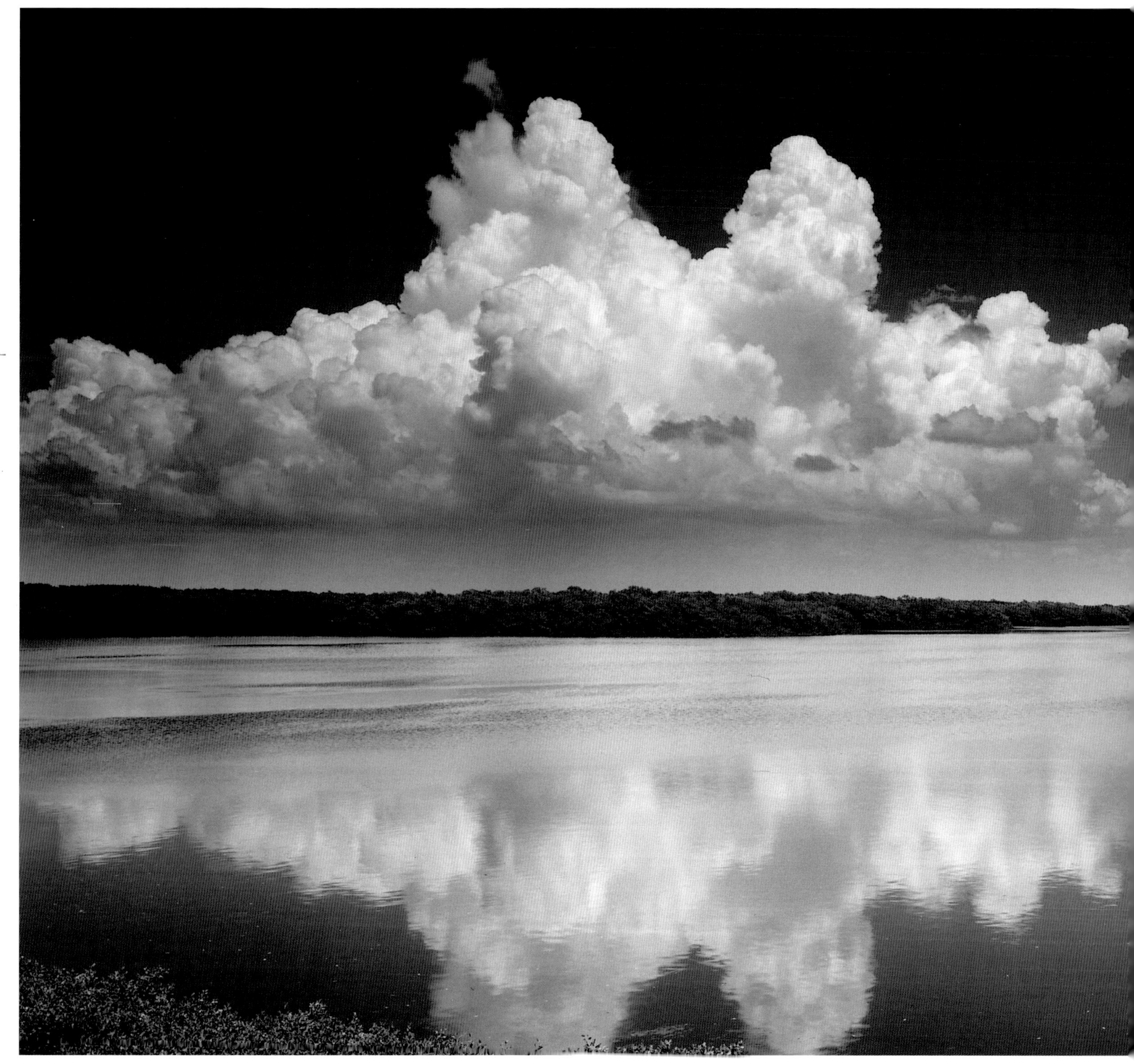

Wilderness Waterway   Plate 35

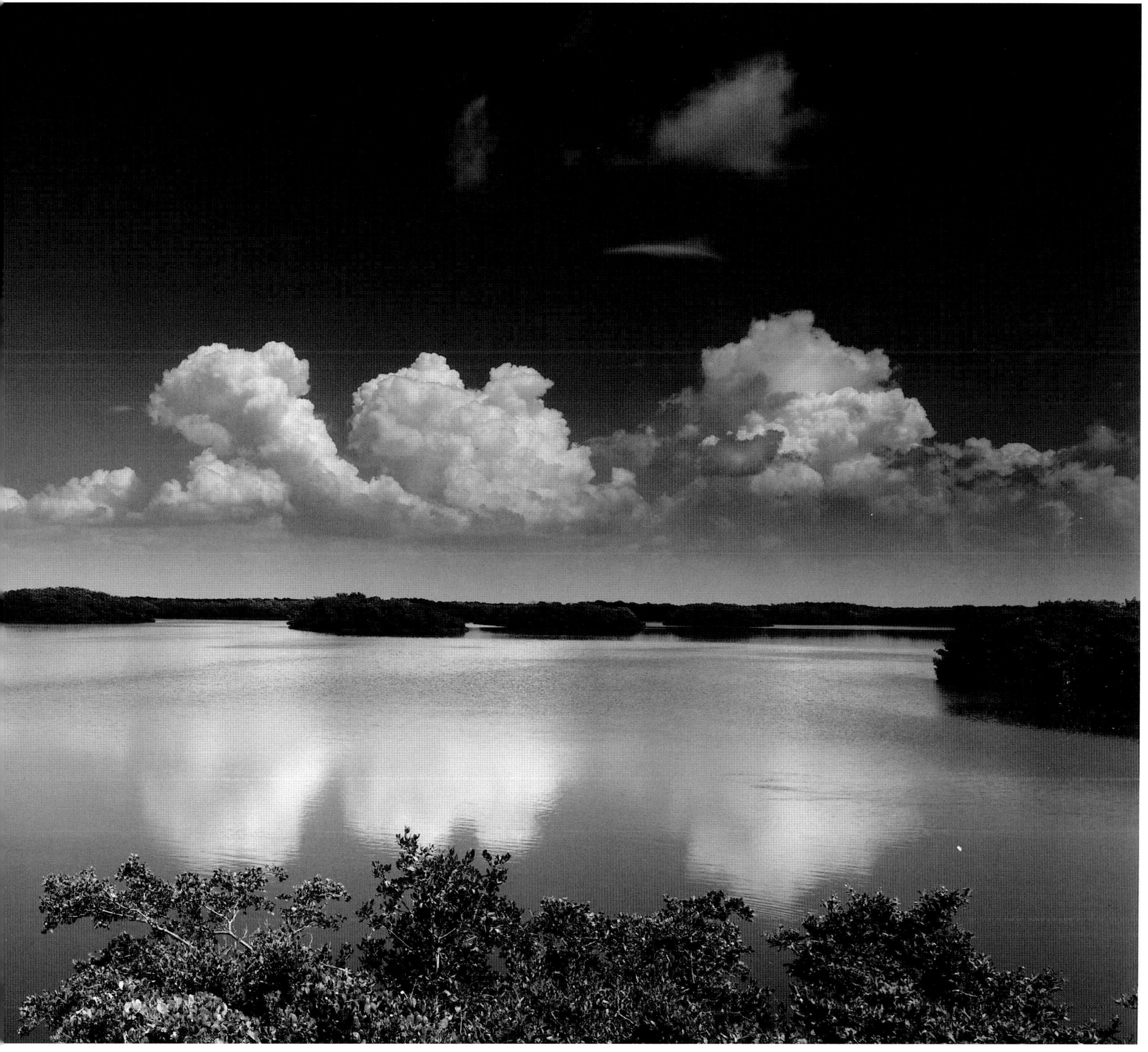

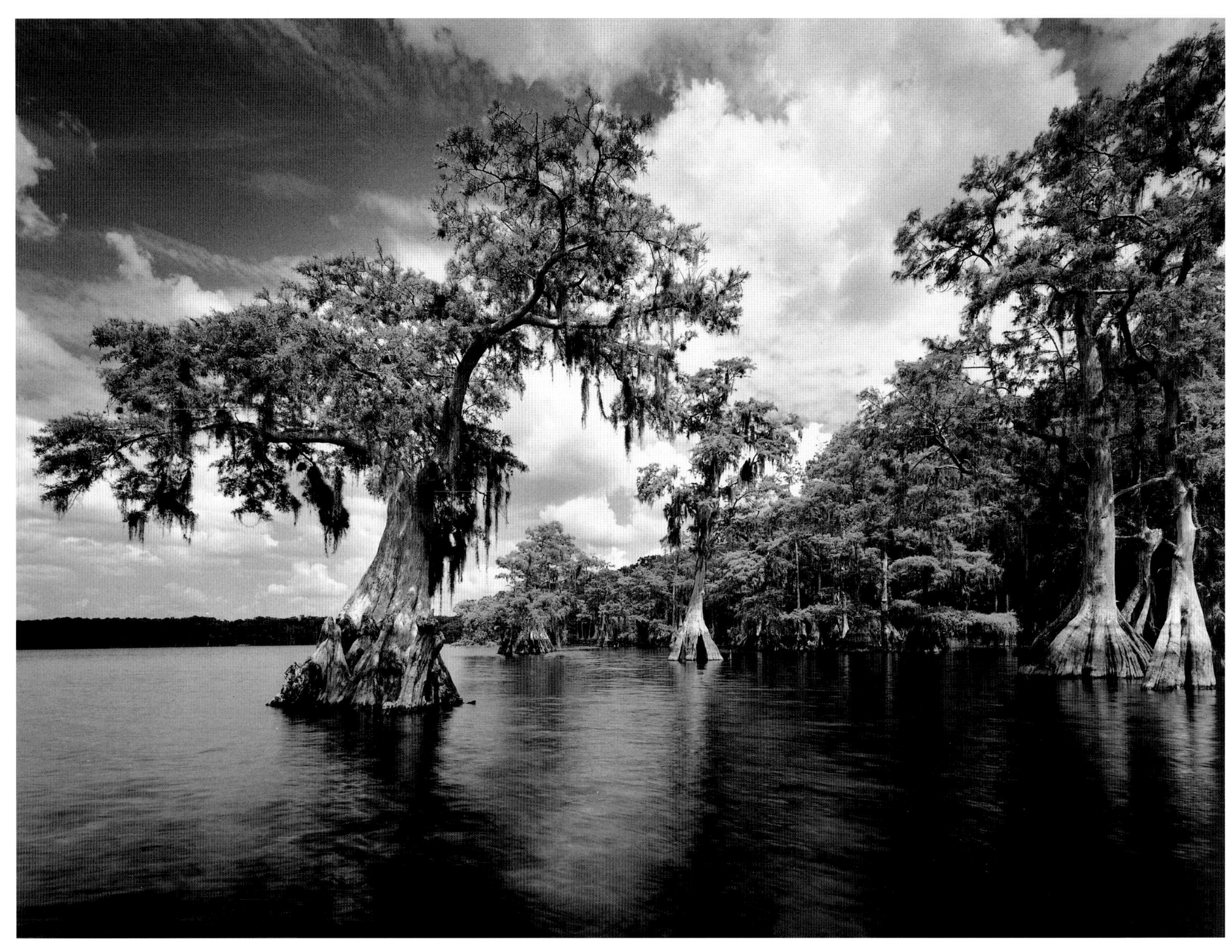

Lake Russell
Plate 36

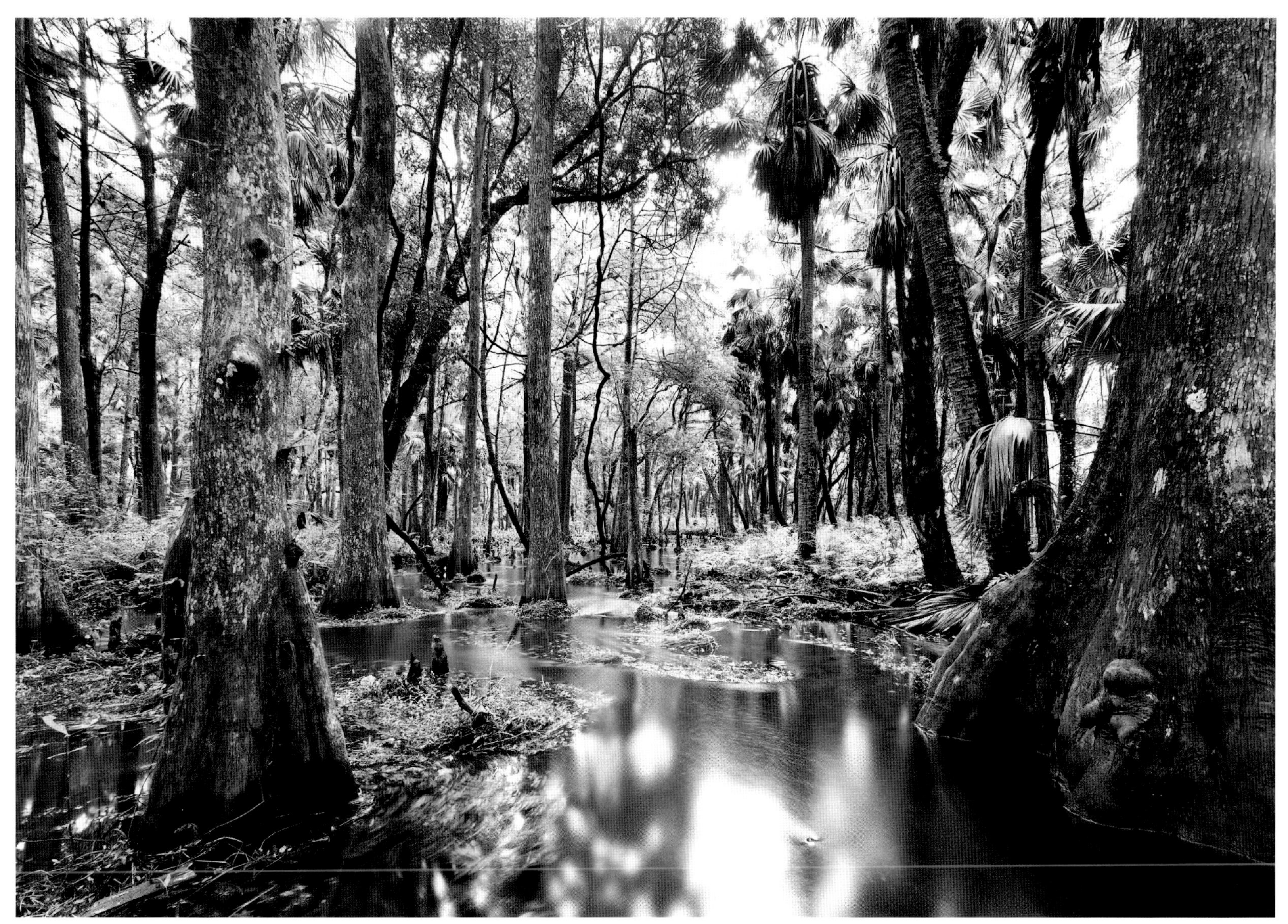

Loxahatchee River #14
Plate 37

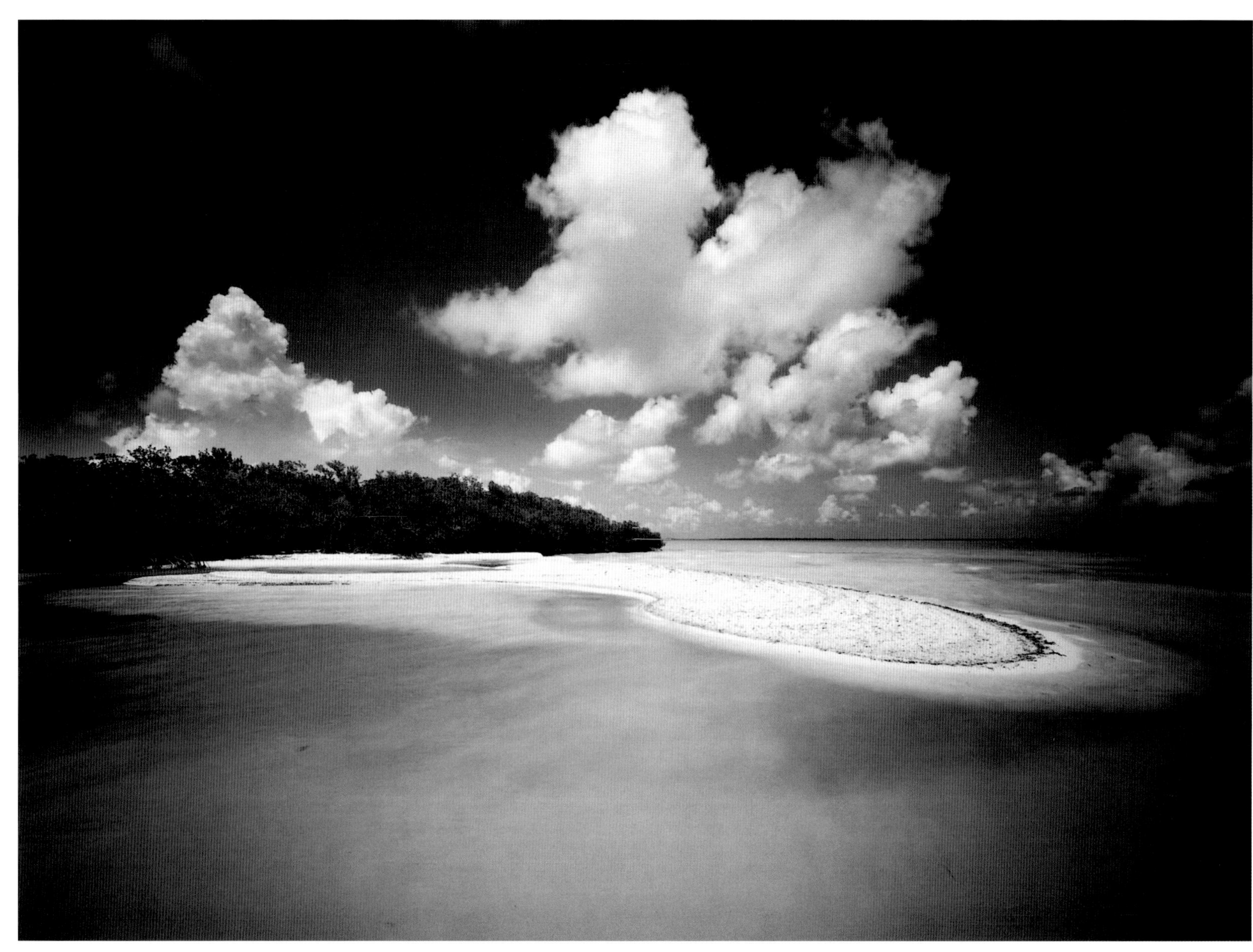

Little Butternut Key #8
Plate 38

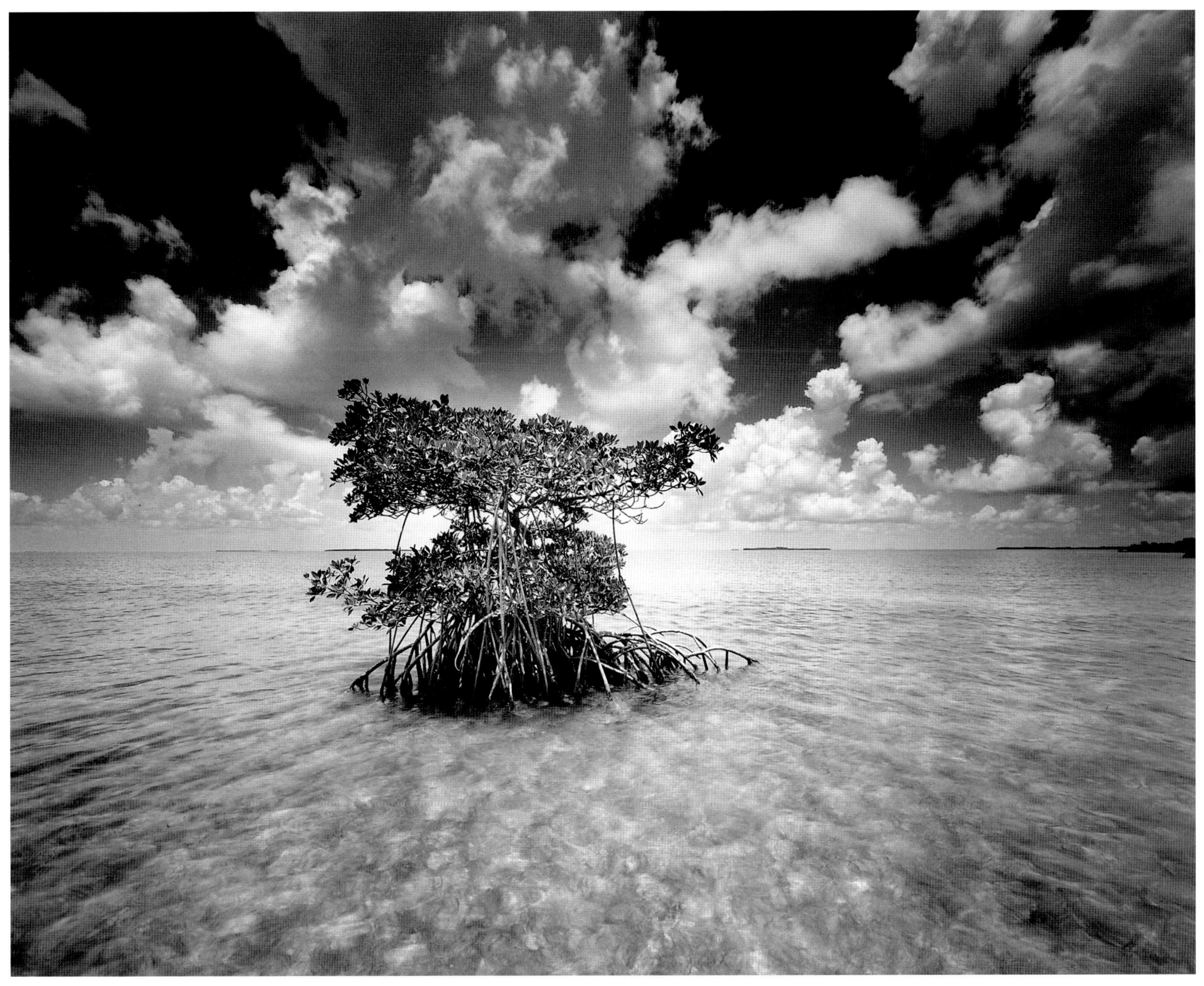

Shell Key #1
Plate 39

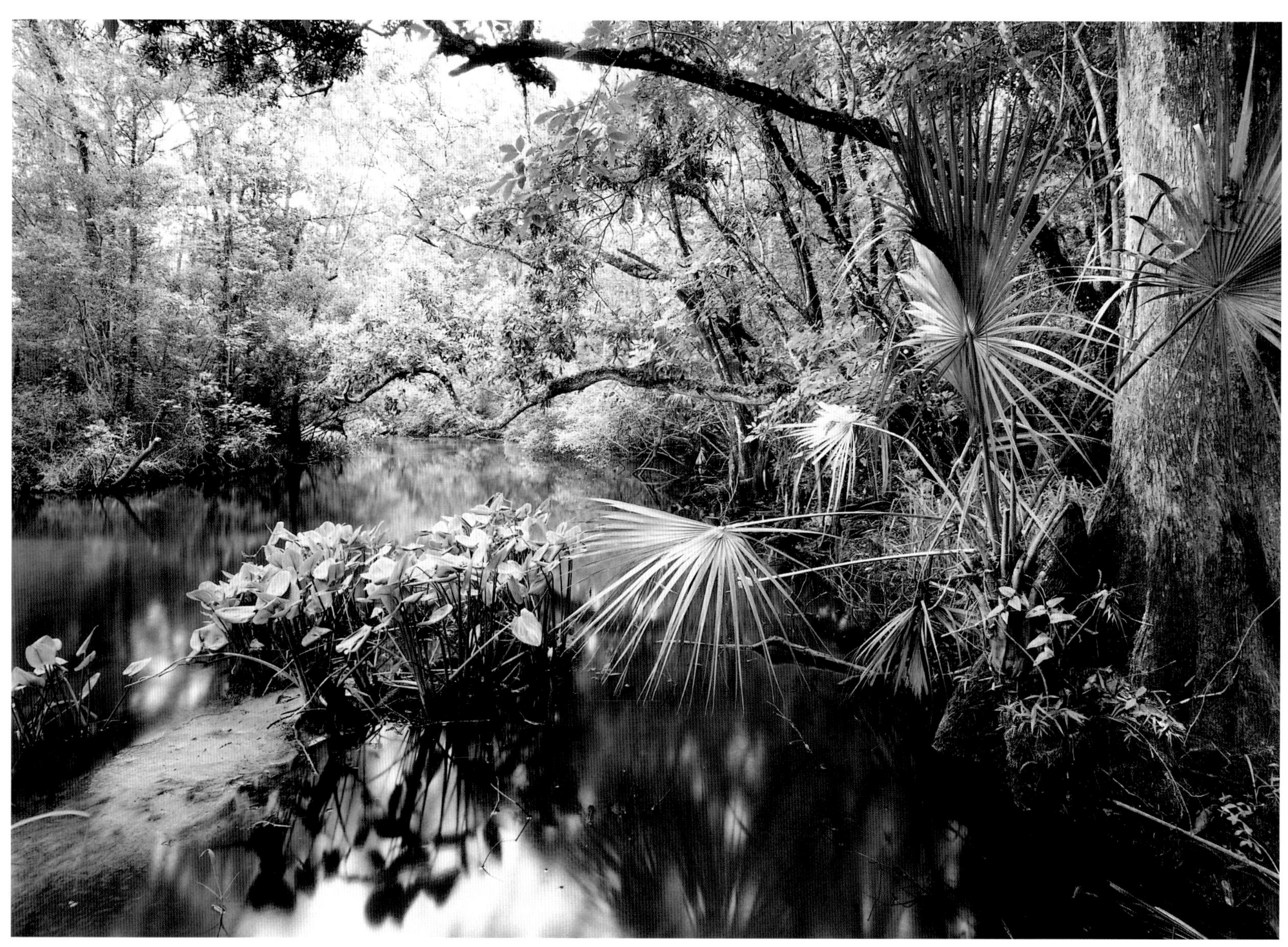

Billies Bay
Plate 40

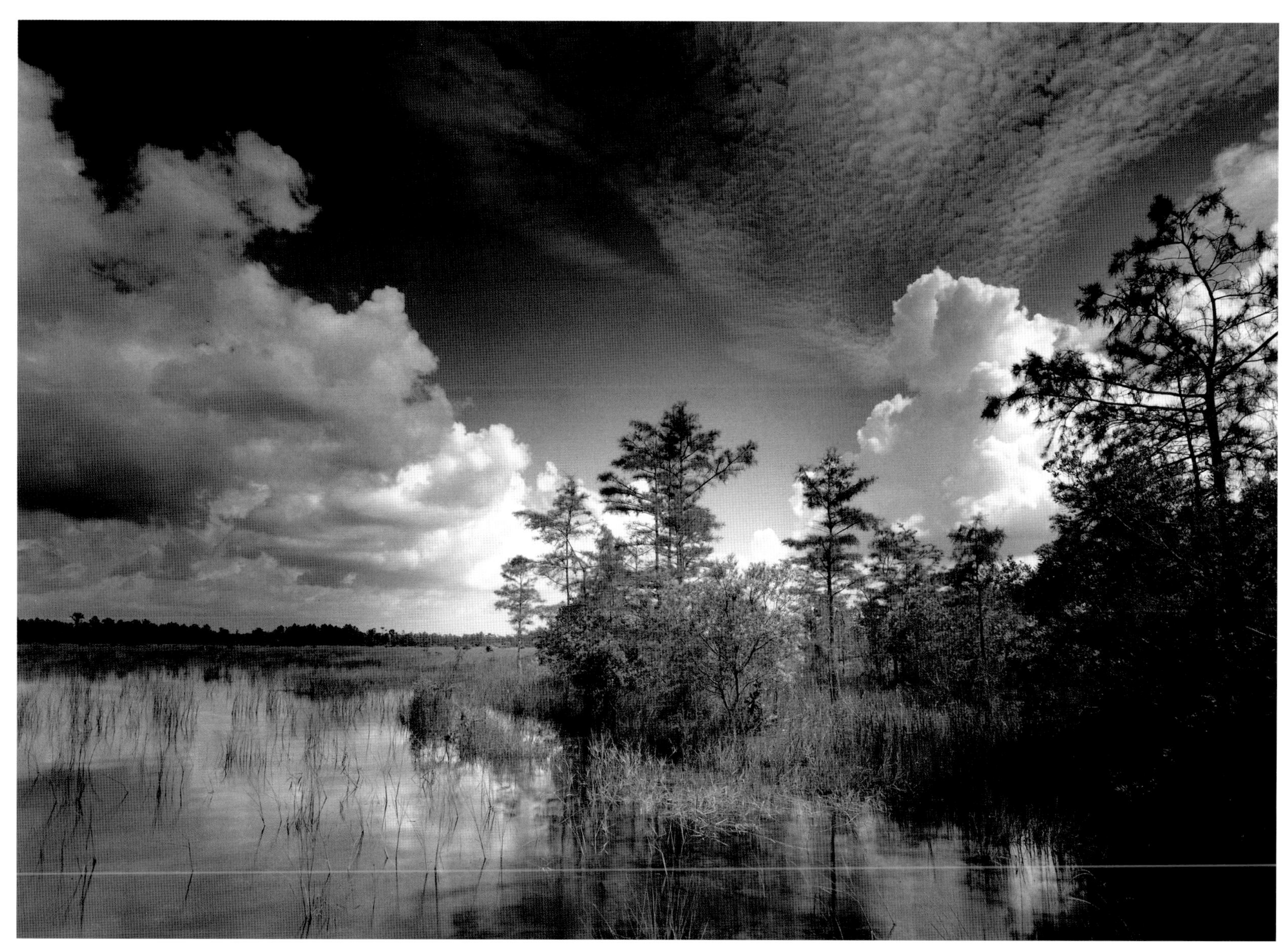

Big Cypress National Preserve #3
Plate 41

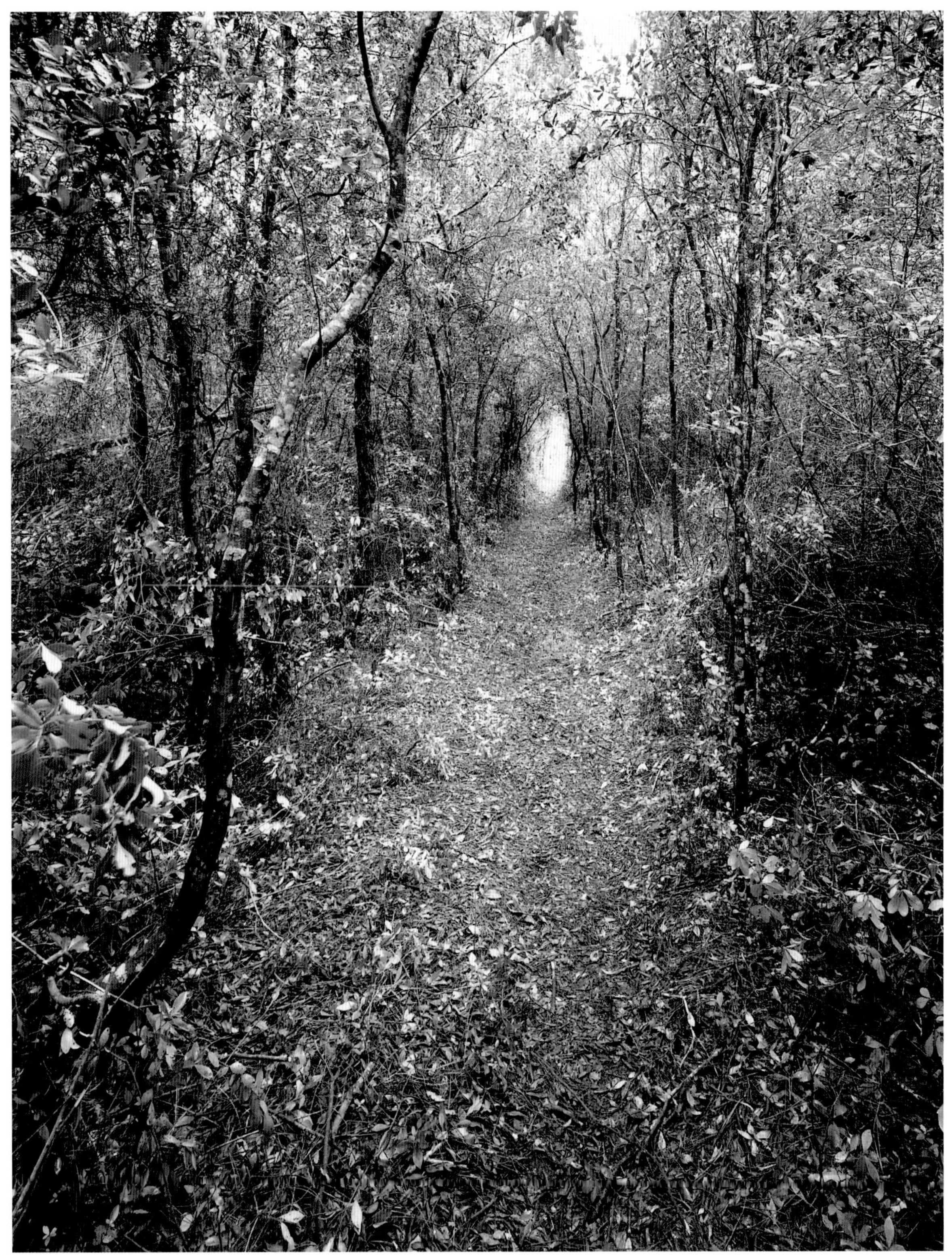

Florida Trail
Plate 42

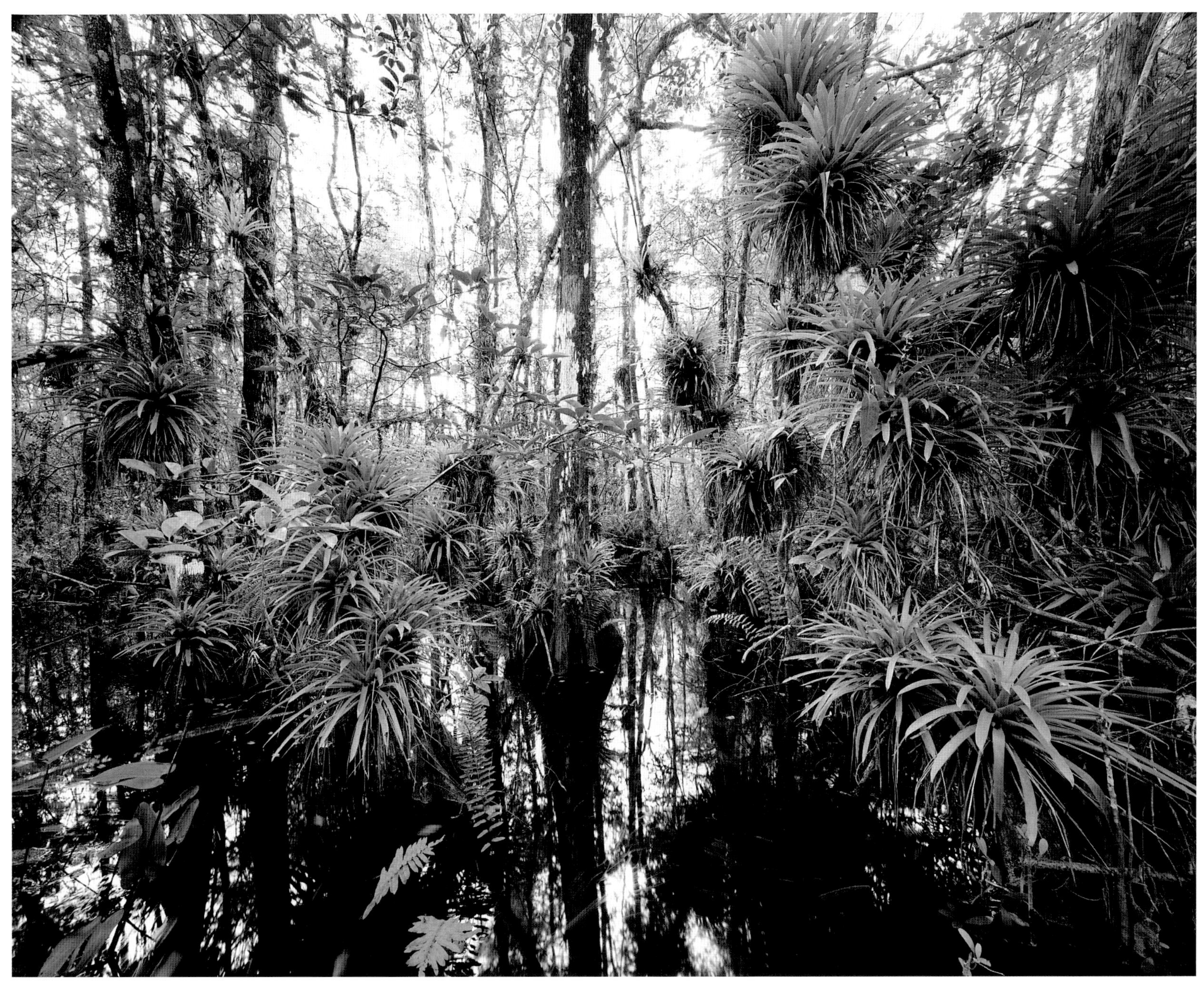

Fakahatchee #3
Plate 43

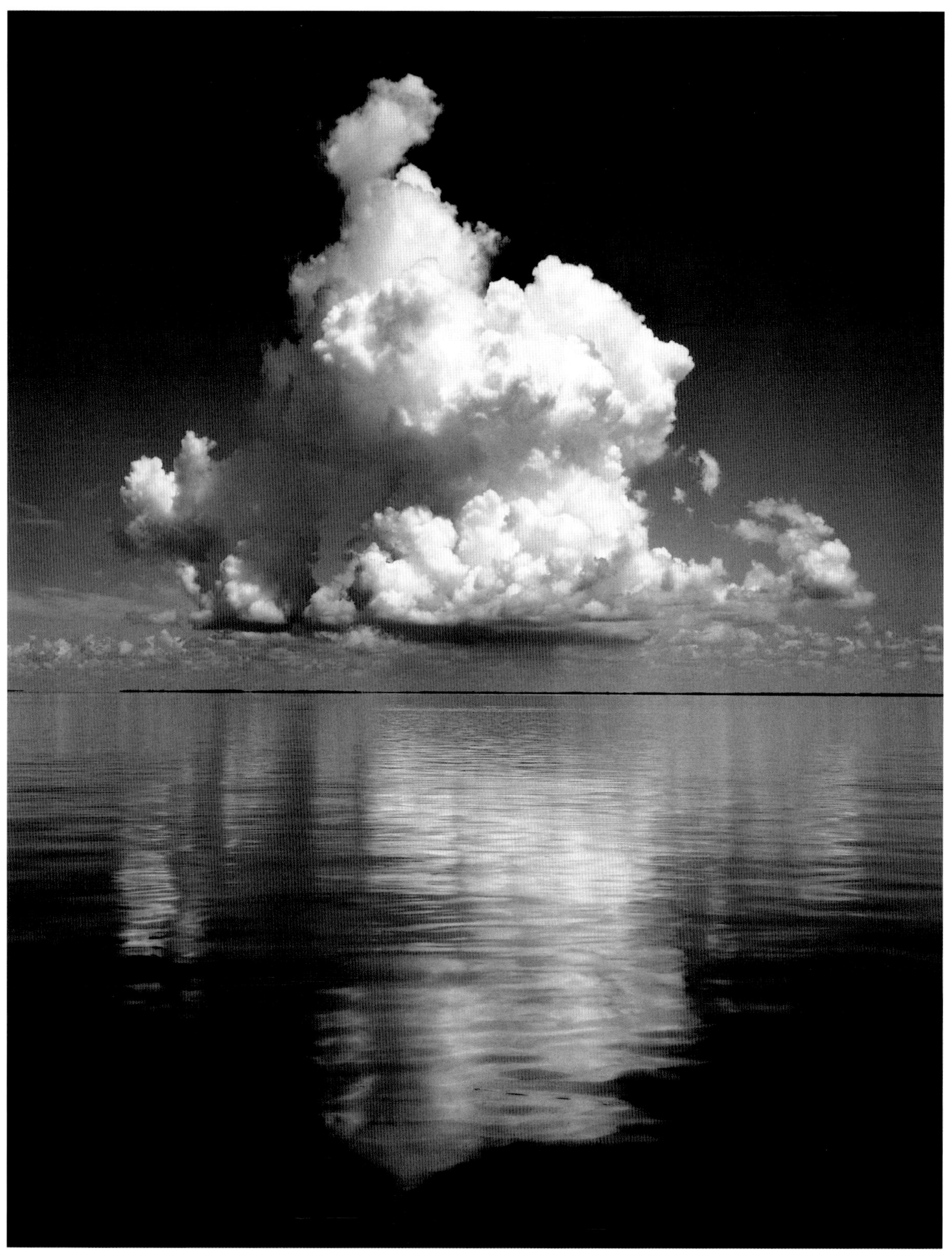

Matlacha Pass
Plate 44

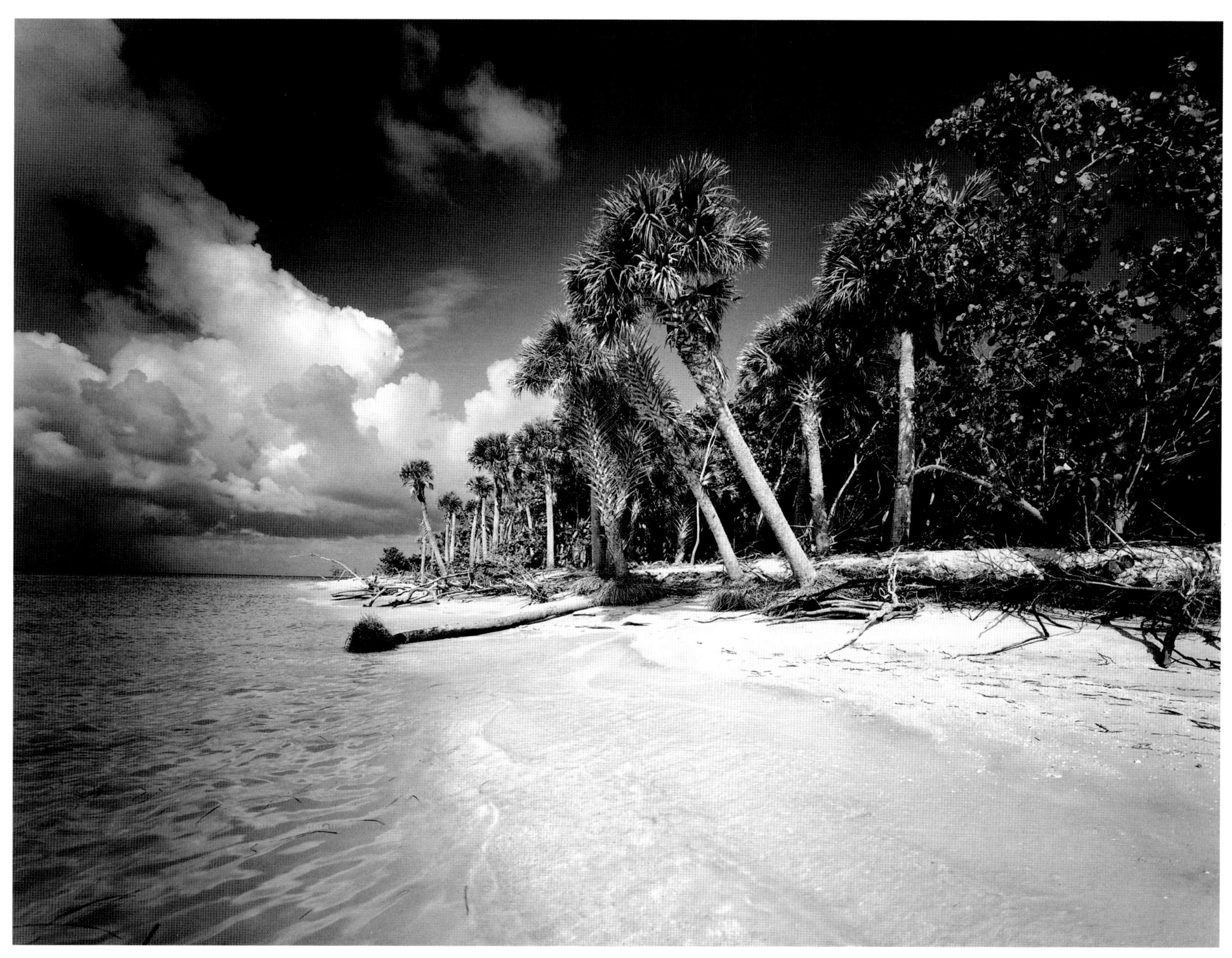

Cayo Costa #3
Plate 45

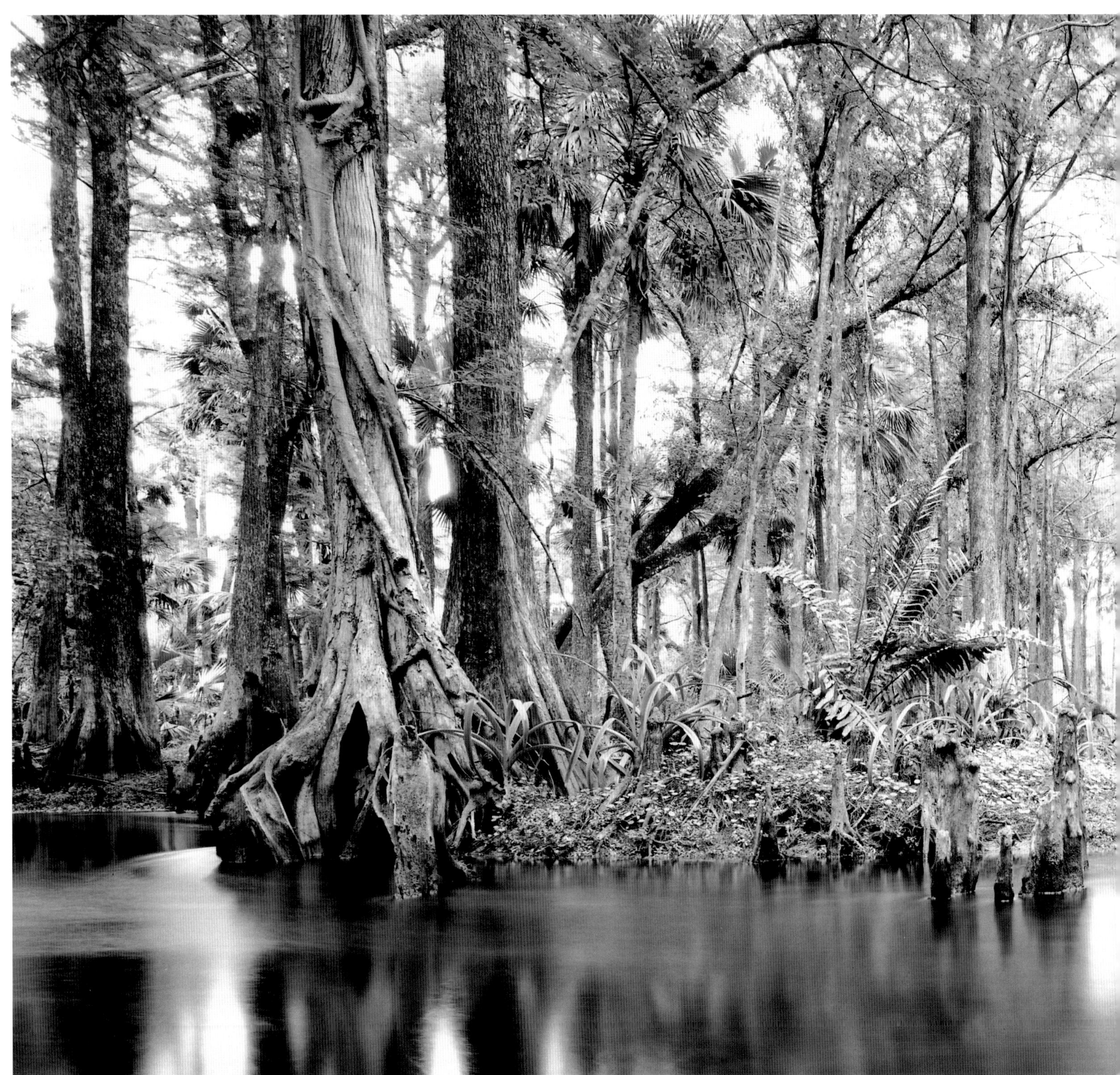

Loxahatchee River #30   Plate 46

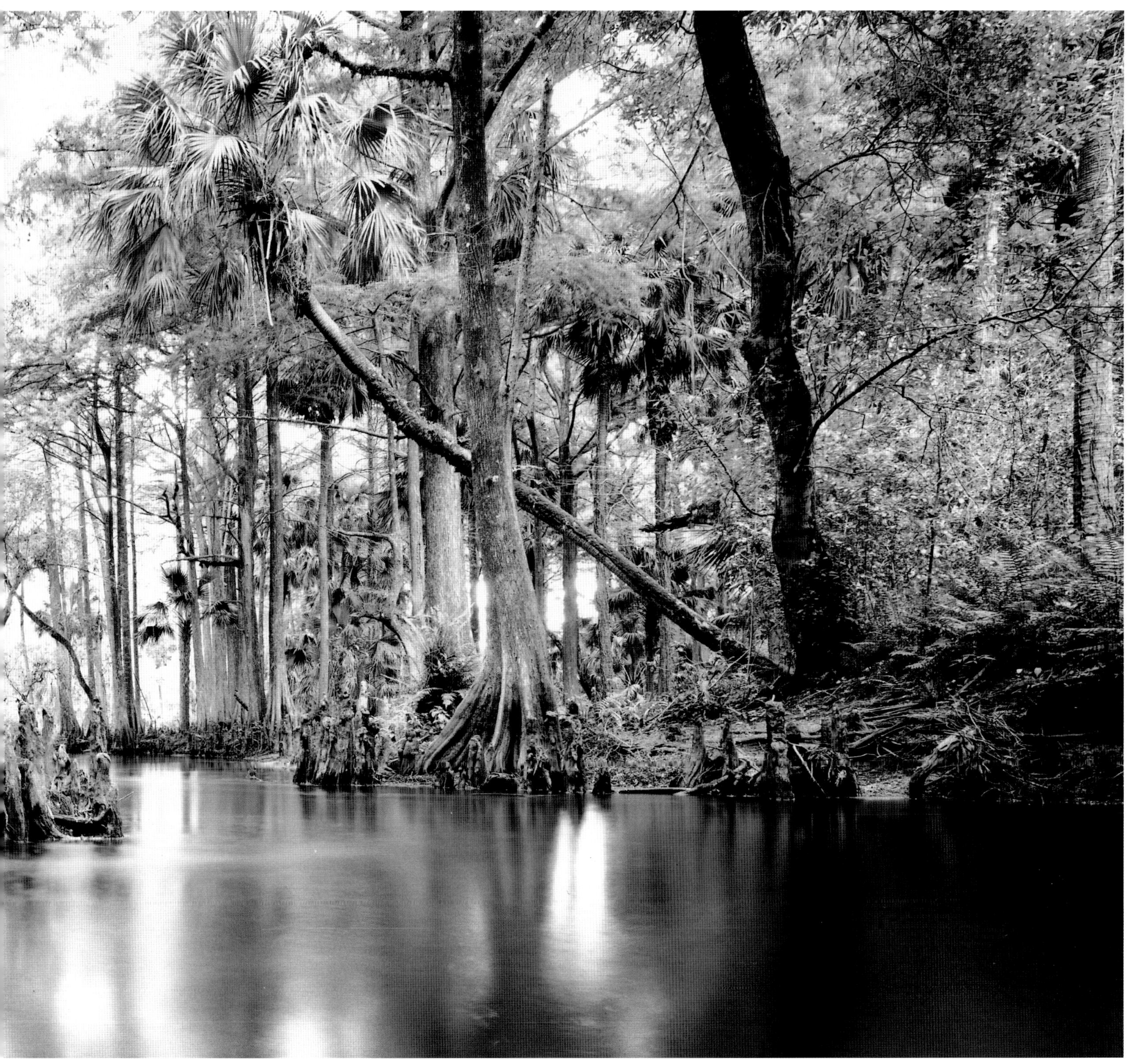

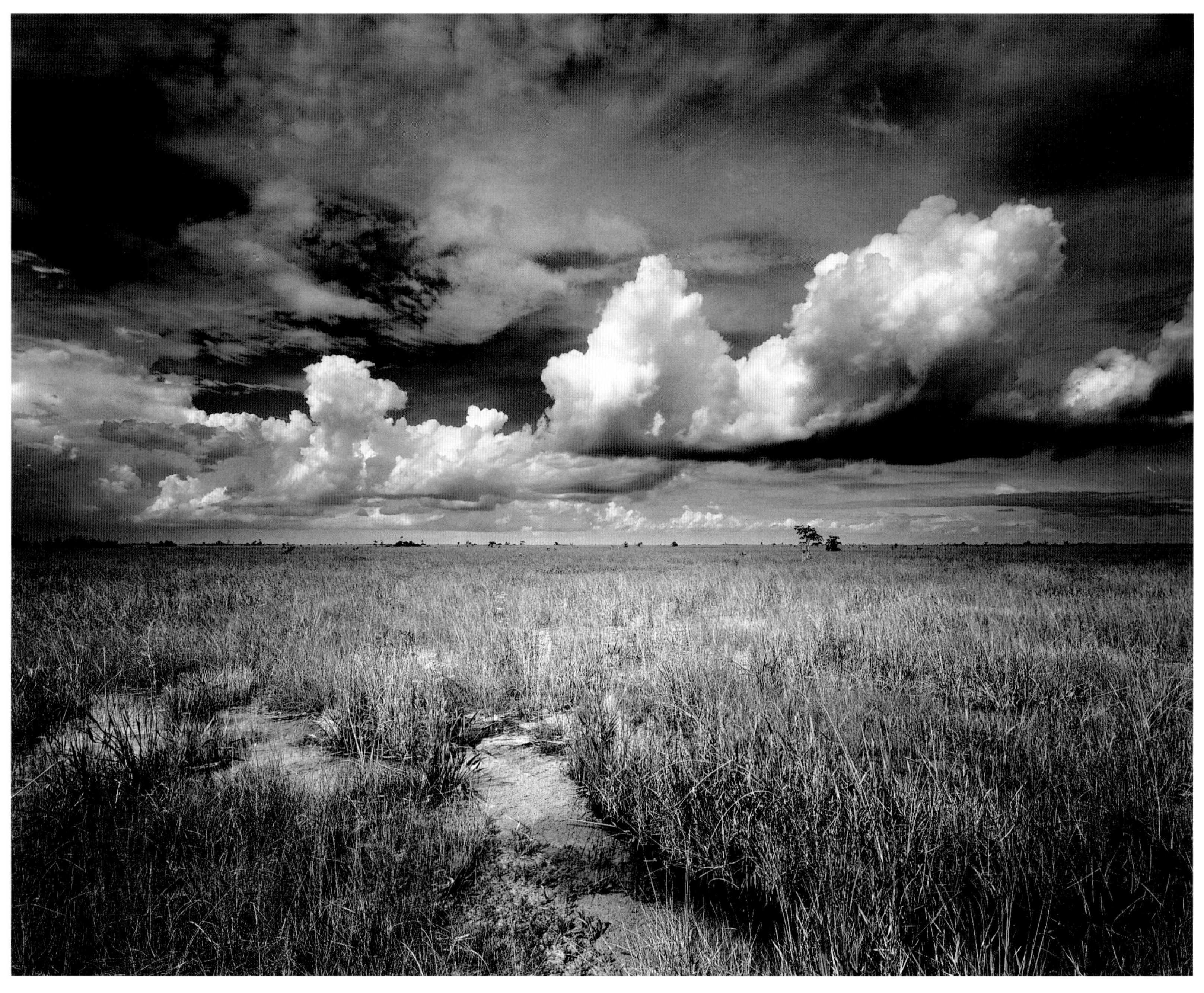

Payhayokee
Plate 47

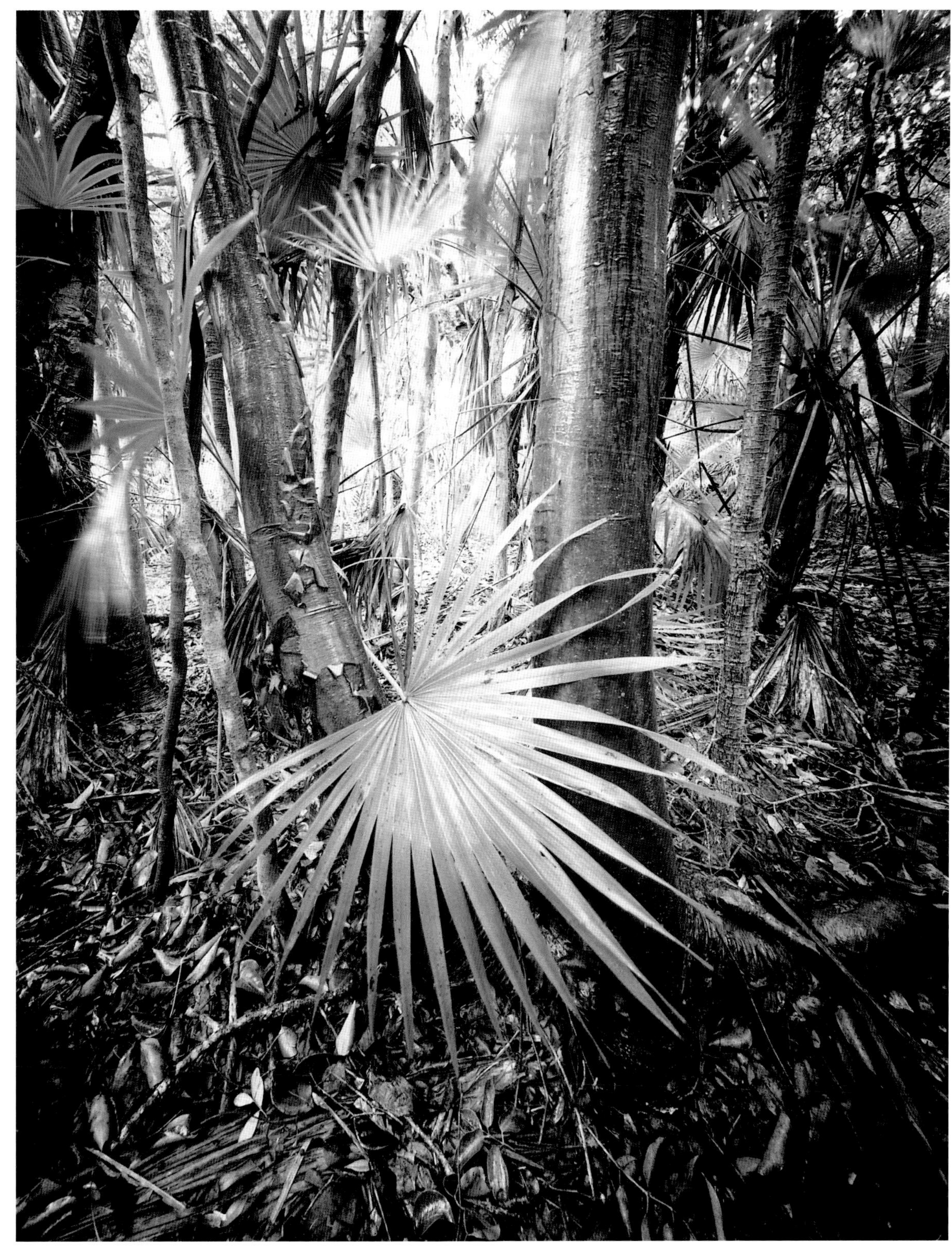

Gumbo Limbo
Plate 48

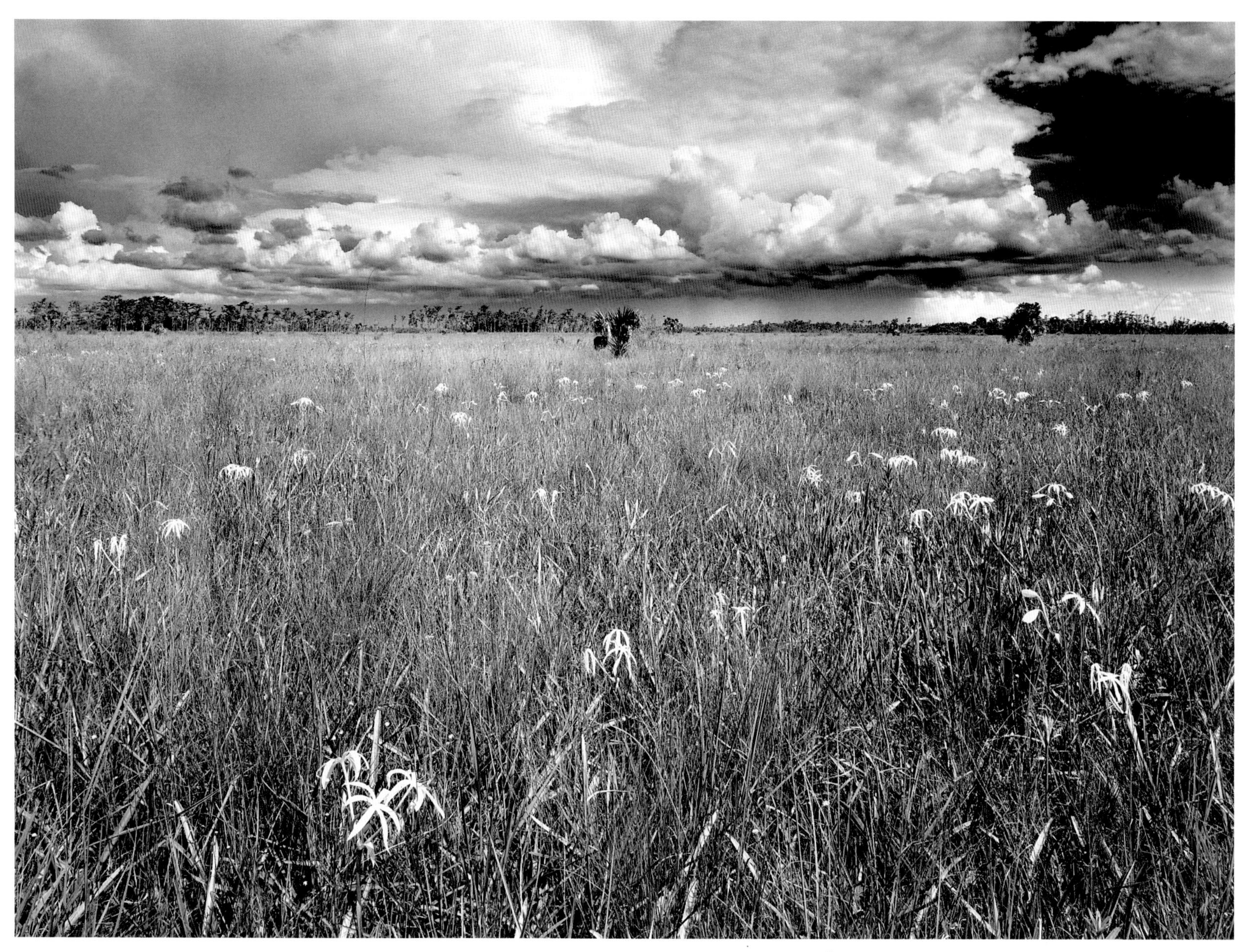

Tamiami Trail #3
Plate 49

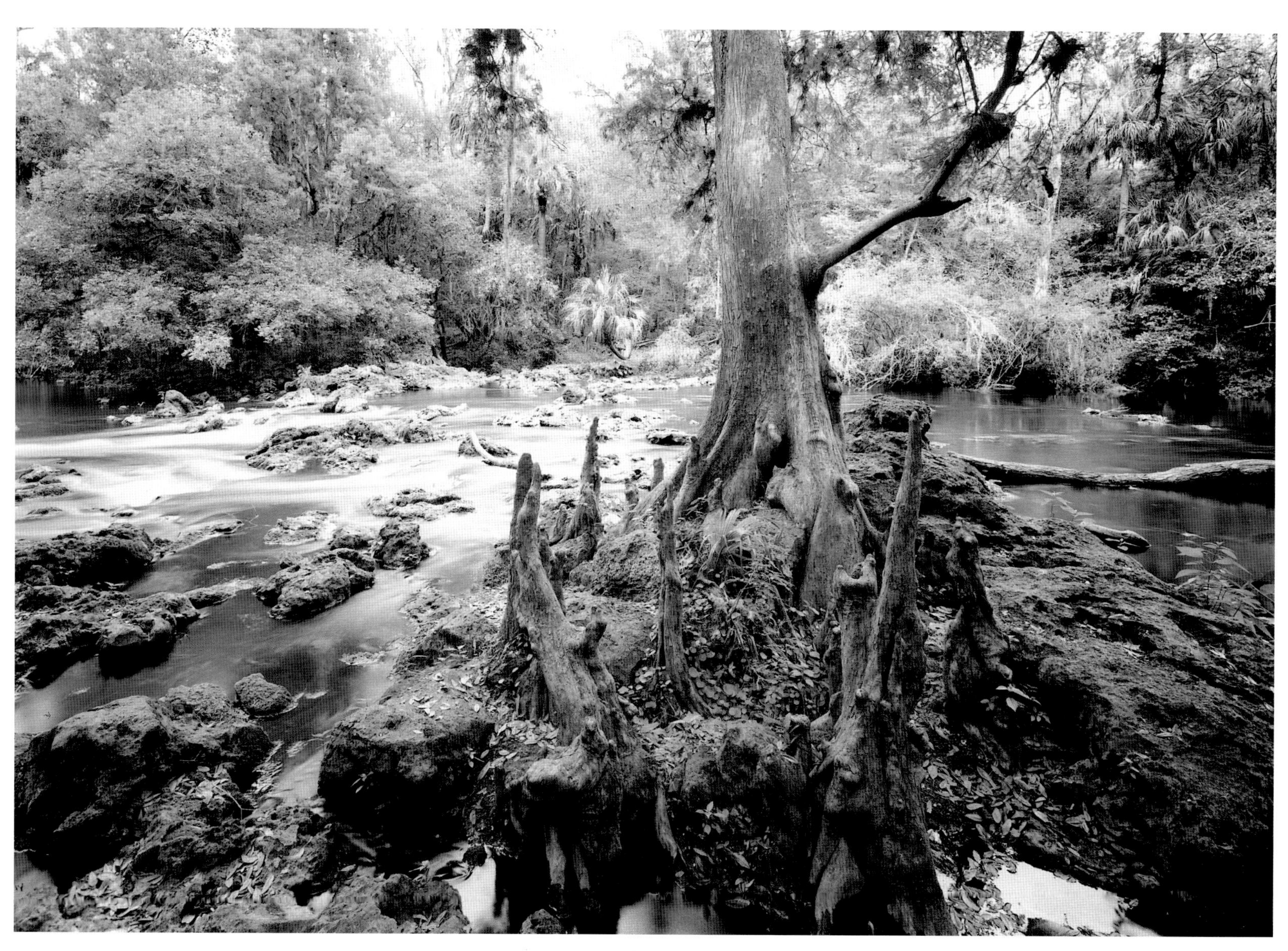

Hillsborough River Rapids
Plate 50

TITLES AND PLATES

Big Cypress Gallery #2 ©1992 - Plate 14
Big Cypress Gallery #14 ©2000 - Plate 30
Big Cypress National Preserve #3 ©1999 - Plate 41
Billies Bay ©1994 - Plate 40
Black Mangrove ©1997 - Plate 34
Blowing Rocks #10 ©1994 - Plate 5
Cayo Costa Island #3 ©1991 - Plate 45
Cody Island ©1991 - Plate 33
Crystal River ©1994 - Plate 19
Everglades Restoration "Can-Do" ©1996 - Plate 29
Fakahatchee Strand #3 ©1999 - Plate 43
Florida Trail ©1994 - Plate 42
Gannet Strand ©1995 - Plate 15
Gaskin #5 ©1998 - Plate 13
Ghost Orchid #1 ©1999 - Plate 21
Ghost Orchid #2 ©1999 - Plate 20
Grand Swamp ©1998 - Plate 12
Gumbo Limbo ©1997 - Plate 48
Hillsborough River Rapids ©1997 - Plate 50
Homosassa Springs ©1999 - Plate 10
Indian Key #5 ©1997 - Plate 17
Indian Key Pass #6 ©1997 - Plate 9
Key Largo Buttonwood #1 ©2001 - Plate 16
Lake Russell ©1998 - Plate 36
Linderman Key ©1997 - Plate #6
Little Butternut Key #1 ©1997 - Plate 25
Little Butternut Key #2 ©1997 - Plate 26
Little Butternut Key #8 ©2001 - Plate 38
Loosescrew Gator ©1996 - Plate 31
Loosescrew Orchid ©1999 - Plate 32
Loosescrew Sanctuary #2 ©1994 - Plate #1
Loxahatchee River #1 ©1991 - Plate 7
Loxahatchee River #7 ©1991 - Plate 23
Loxahatchee River #9 ©1991 - Plate 28
Loxahatchee River #14 ©1991 - Plate 37
Loxahatchee River #30 ©1998 - Plate 46
Matlacha Pass ©1991 - Plate 44
Myakka #5 ©2001 - Plate 4
Myakka Canopy Trail ©2001 - Plate 3
Myakka River #1 ©2000 - Plate 27
Osprey Nest ©1998 - Plate 11
Payhayokee ©1997 - Plate 47
Seven Cabbage Cut ©1991 - Plate 2
Shell Key #1 ©2001 - Plate 39
Skillet Strand ©1996 - Plate 24
Tamiami Trail #2 ©1990 - Plate 8
Tamiami Trail #3 ©1992 - Plate 49
Trout Creek ©1991 - Plate 18
Wagon Wheel Road ©1996 - Plate 22
Wilderness Waterway ©1999 - Plate 35

First published in 2001 by Big Cypress Gallery, 52388 Tamiami Trail, Ochopee, Florida, 34141 (941) 695–2428
Email: mail@clydebutcher.com http://www.clydebutcher.com

2004 printing by University Press of Florida
Printed in China on acid-free paper

10 09 08 07 06 05 6 5 4 3 2 1

A record of cataloging-in-publication data is available from the Library of Congress.
ISBN 0-8130-2825-6

The University Press of Florida is the scholarly publishing agency for the State University System of Florida, comprising Florida A&M University, Florida Atlantic University, Florida Gulf Coast University, Florida International University, Florida State University, University of Central Florida, University of Florida, University of North Florida, University of South Florida, and University of West Florida.

University Press of Florida
15 Northwest 15th Street
Gainesville, FL 32611-2079
http://www.upf.com